MALAYSIA
at Random

Originally published in 2009 by Editions Didier Millet
This edition updated and edited by Justin Corfield

Talisman Publishing Pte Ltd
talisman@apdsing.com
www.talismanpublishing.com

ISBN 978-981-18-8463-4

Copyright © 2009 Editions Didier Millet
Copyright © 2024 Talisman Publishing

The publisher would like to thank Thor Kah Hoong for his assistance with the early drafts for this book and Dato' Mohd Nor bin Khalid (Lat) for permission to reproduce his illustration on p. 110.

All rights reserved. Apart from any fair dealing for the purposes of private study, research, criticism or review as permitted under the Copyright Act, no part of this publication may be reproduced, stored in a retrieval system or transmitted in any form by any means, electronic, mechanical, photocopying, recording or otherwise, without the written permission of the publisher.

Printed in Singapore

Disclaimer:
Whilst every effort has been made to ensure that the information contained in this book is accurate for a book of entertainment and enjoyment, in the event of errors or omissions, if relevant, appropriate credit will be made in future printing of this work.

magic, myths
& milestones

TALISMAN

When you are abroad and missing home, what do you miss most? ...You yearn for Penang laksa at a midnight stall, midmorning roadside rojak and instant iced cendol on sweltering afternoons.

You miss the chant of the kacang putih man and the goreng pisang boy, the Hindustani tunes sung in Malay and Chinese, the roar of an East coast storm, the matchless din of Malaysian markets, and young voices saying, "Aiya! Whole life study, matilah!"

—Adibah Amin, *As I Was Passing*

THE OLDEST PERSON IN MALAYSIA?

There were two small rebellions against the British. One was led by Mat Kilau in Pahang in 1891-95. The other, led by Tok Janggut, aged 62, was in Kelantan in 1915. The British reported various accounts of the death of Mat Kilau in 1895 and 1896, and in June 1915 after defeating the rebels in Kelantan, the British displayed a body that they claimed at Tok Janggut, before it was buried in Kota Bharu.

In December 1969, a person in Pulau Tawar, Pahang, stated that he was Mat Kilau. A committee investigated the claims and found that the elderly man in Pahang was Mat Kilau, aged 103. Before his death in August 1970, Mat Kilau mentioned that he had met Tok Janggut in 1966. If true, Tok Janggut would have been aged around 113.

The oldest living person in Malaysia is Annamah Abukutty, born on 31 March 1911 in India, aged 111. Mahathir bin Mohamad when he became Prime Minister for the second time, in 2018, was, at the age of 92 years and 141 days, the oldest prime minister in the world.

PRIME MINISTERS AND FOOTBALL

Tunku Abdul Rahman	Member of the Penang Free School junior football team.
Tun Abdul Razak	Wing forward in the Raffles College football team.
Tun Hussein Onn	Captain of the English College Johore Bahru football team.
Tun Abdullah Badawi	His father was a founder of the football club Malaya Hijaz in Saudi Arabia.
Dato' Sri Najib Tun Razak	Played football at Malvern College, England, and a supporter of Manchester United Football Club.
Dato Sri Ismail Sabri Yaacob	A supporter of Chelsea Football Club.

ORIGINS OF THE "FIVE FOOT WAY"

"All houses constructed of brick or tiles have a common type of front each having an arcade of a certain depth, open to all sides as a continuous and open passage on each side of the street."

— *Sir Stamford Raffles' instructions to the Town Planning Committee of Singapore, 1822*

MATERIALS NEEDED TO BUILD A BASIC KAMPONG HOUSE

- Lengths of hardwood (e.g. chengal)
- Strips of bamboo
- Woven *attap* or galvanised iron sheets
- Reinforced concrete bases

SELECTING AN AUSPICIOUS SITE FOR A KAMPONG HOUSE

- A *bomoh* (traditional Malay healer) chants blessings and burns incense at the site.
- The *ibu rumah* (woman of the house) measures both a stick and string of rattan to the length of her outstretched arms.
- The *bomoh* ties the string of rattan to the stick and plants it at the site next to a bucket of water with a dish underneath it.
- The next morning at dawn, the *ibu rumah* measures the length of the stick and string of rattan and checks the water. If the stick or string has lengthened, or if the water has overflowed into the dish, the site is chosen.
- The site, if chosen, becomes the exact spot where the *tiang seri* (main post) is erected. It is believed that the *semangat rumah* (spirit of the house) resides in the *tiang seri*.

MALAYSIAN SIGN LANGUAGE

Also known as Kod Tangan Bahasa Malaysia or Manually Coded Malay, Malaysian Sign Language was implemented for the teaching of Malay in schools for the hearing impaired in 1985.

perdana menteri (prime minister)   **Ipoh**   **Malacca**   **Sarawak**

HOW TO ARTIFICIALLY INSEMINATE AN ASIAN ELEPHANT

1. Monitor the female elephant's oestrous cycle—each cycle lasts four months—and identify the specific hormone surge that causes ovulation.
2. Collect semen from the male elephant 12 to 24 hours before the insemination procedure is due to begin.
3. Bathe the female in warm, soapy water, and then give a warm water enema to cleanse the rectum.
4. Place the female under ultrasound to visualise its reproductive tract.
5. Guide a catheter through the tract, and deposit semen directly into the cervix or uterus.

IT'S A BIRD, IT'S A PLANE

Official Malaysian *wau* (kite) competition rules

1. The competition field must comprise a minimum area of 75 x 120 metres.
2. The frame and *dengung* (hammer) of the *wau* must be made using natural materials found in the country.
3. Contestants are free to use any type of paper to make their *wau*.
4. The *wau's* wingspan must measure 1.2 metres and the string should be at least 1,000 metres in length.
5. All *wau* must be registered and certified before the beginning of the contest.
6. If the *wau* falls within the specified time frame, it can be flown again, provided that only the two members of the *wau* team are involved in repairing and raising it again.
7. Marks will be awarded by the judges according to the following criteria:

a. Height	40 marks
b. Overall beauty	30 marks
- Design creativity	
- Patterns/decorations	
c. Perseverance in the air	20 marks
d. Hammer (vibrating and humming sound)	10 marks
Total	**100 marks**

Source: *Traditional Kites of Malaysia* by Muzium Layang-Layang Pasir Gudang, 2002

HOW TO PRAY AT A MALAYSIAN HINDU TEMPLE

1. Before entering the temple, remove your shoes, wash your feet, especially the heels, and sprinkle water over your head.
2. Enter the temple. If you are a man, stand on the left. If you are a woman, stand on the right.
3. Present offerings—flowers, garlands or fruits—to the statue of the main deity.
4. Put your palms together and utter a chant or prayer.
5. When a priest comes with a camphor lamp, put your hands over the flames and then touch your eyes.
6. When a priest comes with a white powder (made from cow dung), apply some of the powder with your finger onto your forehead between your eyes. Do the same thing when the priest offers you saffron paste and *kum kum* (turmeric with slaked lime).
7. When a priest comes with the holy water and spoons it into the palm of your hand, drink it.
8. For RM3, buy an offering comprising a coconut, flowers and fruits as well as areca nuts (also known as betel nuts), leaves and cow dung powder and, holding the offering, circle the statue of the main deity three (or any odd number of) times.
9. Kneel in front of the statue of the main deity and bow, knocking your head lightly on the ground.
10. If you want to make an additional prayer, buy a coconut for RM1 and break it on the ground or light it with a piece of camphor, and then circle it in front of your face clockwise three times and anti-clockwise three times, and then break it on the ground.
11. If you want to make an additional prayer, buy a small oil lamp made of clay for RM1 and place it in front of the statue of the main deity.

WHAT'S IN THE BAG?

The traditional Malay medicine bag carried by a *bomoh* (traditional Malay healer) is yellow (symbolising the Malay rulers' power) and may contain:

- roots
- ten white pearl-sized stones
- pieces of sulphur
- the gall bladder of a bear
- the nest of a white sparrow
- an amulet, usually a talismanic symbol written in saffron ink on a brown wooden plate, which protects the medicine in the bag
- the bones of various animals

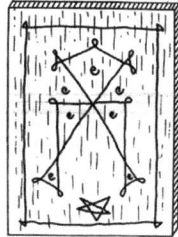

Source: *Royal Healer* by Roland Werner, 2002

HOW THE KUALA LUMPUR SMART TUNNEL WORKS

First mode (normal conditions)
Under normal conditions (when there is no storm), no floodwater is diverted into the system and traffic can flow normally.

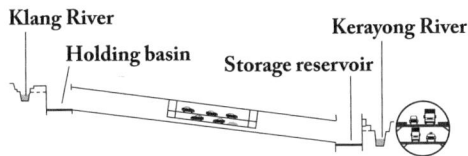

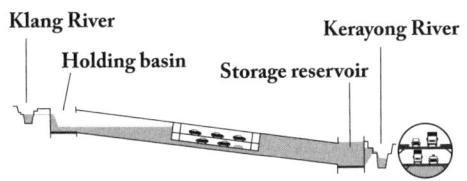

Second mode (most storms)
When the second mode is activated, floodwater is diverted into the bypass tunnel in the lower channel of the motorway tunnel. The motorway section is still open to traffic at this stage.

Third mode (major storms)
When the third mode is in operation, the motorway will be closed to all traffic. After making sure all vehicles have exited the motorway, automated watertight gates will be opened to allow floodwater to pass through. The motorway will be reopened to traffic within 48 hours of closure.

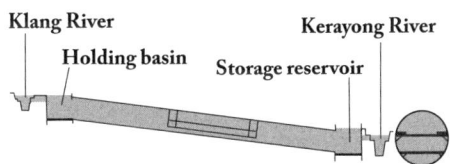

Source: SMART

ZOO NEGARA MALAYSIA

Zoo Negara, the national zoo, has its origins in a miniature zoo set up by Victor Hutson at the Malayan Agri-Horticultural Association (MAHA) exhibition in 1958. When they were not at the exhibition, Hutson's animals were kept at his five-acre garden in the Bangsar Estate (now Damansara). Among the animals were an Indo–Chinese tiger named Nikky, three orang-utans named Jacko, Suzan and Jane and six estuarine crocodiles. The popularity of Hutson's exhibit led to the founding of Zoo Negara, which was officially opened in 1963. In 2009, Zoo Negara boasts a total of 5,137 animals from 479 species of mammals, birds, reptiles, amphibians and fish.

Number of Bridges in Putrajaya: still

SOME PERFORMANCE PROBLEMS IN MALAYSIA

Year	Artists	Issue	Resolution
2022	**Justin Bieber**	He cancels a show after worries concerning facial paralysis.	After a recovery, he does perform.
2021	**Ramli Ibrahim**	He was going to present an online talk about how multicultural performing arts should transcend race.	Universiti Teknologi Malaysia cancelled it for 'undisclosed reasons'.
2013	**Ke$ha**	She was going to perform in Kuala Lumpur.	She refused to change show to comply with local culture, and it was cancelled.
2009	**Rihanna**	Local religious and political groups protested against the artist's provocative attire.	Rihanna agreed to comply with the fashion restrictions, but the concert was postponed due to her own personal problems.
2008	**Avril Lavigne**	She was deemed "too sexy" for Malaysian audiences by local religious and political groups.	Lavigne complied with the regulations, and the concert went ahead.
2008	**Inul Daratista**	Local religious and political groups protested against the Indonesian *dangdut* singer's trademark hip gyrations, called "*gelek gerudi*".	Authorities in Kuala Lumpur and Johor cancelled her concert permits, and her shows were called off.
2007	**Beyoncé**	Local religious and political groups sought to compel Beyoncé to adhere to strict guidelines on dress and performance.	Beyoncé cancelled her show.
2004	**Mariah Carey**	Local religious and political groups said that Mariah's attire and style of performance were not appropriate for local audiences.	Mariah agreed to comply with local regulations and went ahead with her concert.
2003	**Linkin Park**	Local religious and political groups protested against the rock band, fearing that their wild stage antics would be a negative influence on the country's youth.	The band agreed not to scream, jump around, use vulgar language, wear shorts, or make obscene gestures on stage, and the concert went ahead.

1996	**Michael Jackson**	The Selangor state government refused to grant a permit to Michael Jackson, fearing his hip gyrations and pelvic thrusts would be a bad influence on the country's youth.	The concert went ahead in Kuala Lumpur instead of Selangor.
1990	**LaToya Jackson and Atlantic Starr**	The Cultural Division of the Culture and Tourism Ministry withdrew their approval because they discovered that LaToya had posed semi-nude in *Playboy* magazine in 1989. Atlantic Starr, another act which was supposed to perform in the *Kent Night of Nights Concert*, decided to exclude Malaysia from its tour route after the incident.	The *Kent Night of Nights Concert* went ahead without LaToya Jackson and Atlantic Starr. They were replaced by local band Made in Malaysia and American group, Fratband.
1965	**Les Ballets Africains**	The African women in the show danced bare-breasted.	The Malaysian police previewed the ballet and declared that it was not obscene. The show went on with one condition imposed—that there be an announcement before each performance that this was a cultural show from Africa.

IDENTIFYING MALAYSIA AIRLINES STAFF

Female staff
- **In-flight supervisors:** batik *sarong kebaya* of ottanio blue colour with yellow flowers.
- **Chief stewardesses, leading stewardesses and flight stewardesses:** batik *sarong kebaya* of ottanio blue colour with pink flowers.
- **Ground front-liners:** batik *sarong kebaya* of ottanio blue colour with magenta flowers.

Male staff
- **In-flight supervisors, chief stewards, leading stewards and flight stewards:** dark shade ottanio blue colour jackets.
- **Ground front-liners:** light shade ottanio blue colour jackets.

TRADITIONAL SILAT STYLE

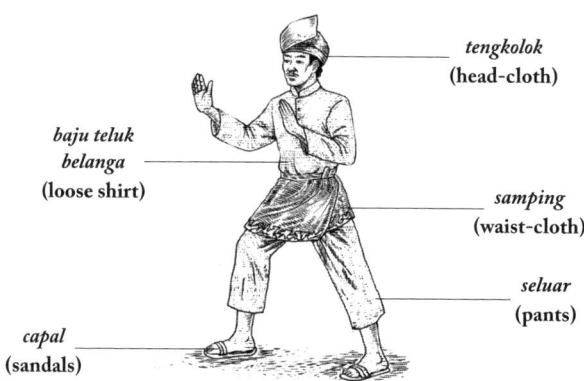

HOW TO COLLECT SWIFTLETS' NESTS IN THE NIAH CAVES, SARAWAK

1. Sacrifice a chicken or goat at the entrance of the cave to appease the spirits of the cave and to ensure a bountiful harvest.
2. Lay a fishing net above the stream that flows in the cave to prevent the nests from dropping into it.
3. Climb up a 20–50-metre bamboo pole to reach a collecting platform at the top of the cave.
4. Using a three-metre socketed bamboo stem with a hoe-shaped iron head and a light bulb at the tip, scrape the nests from the cave ceiling.
5. Let the nests fall to the cave floor where another collector will pick them up.

HOW TO PROCESS A PREMIUM-GRADE BLACK BIRDS' NEST

1. Soak the nest in water for 12 to 48 hours.
2. Using a pair of tweezers, separate the feathers from the nest.
3. To remove fine and deeply embedded feathers, swirl the nest in a circular container containing a few drops of vegetable oil.
4. Rearrange the meaty portions of the nest into a diamond-shaped mould.
5. Allow the moist birds' nest chips to dry.

SOME LAWS YOU SHOULD KNOW ABOUT

2(a) Any person, not being a member of the armed forces of Malaysia or of a visiting force, who wears any camouflage uniform or any part thereof or anything resembling a camouflage uniform or has in his possession, custody or control camouflage cloth or camouflage uniform or any part thereof or anything resembling any camouflage cloth shall be guilty of an offence and shall be liable on conviction to a fine not exceeding 500 ringgit or to imprisonment for a term not exceeding 6 months or to both.

11(b) Any person who rides or leads any elephant on any public road without the permission of the Chief Police Officer or of an officer authorised by him shall be liable to a fine not exceeding 50 ringgit.

15(d) Any person who spits in any coffee shop, eating house, school premises or public place or in any trolley-bus, omnibus, railway carriage or other public conveyance or in or near any public road shall be liable to a fine not exceeding 100 ringgit. Provided that nothing in this paragraph shall prohibit any person from spitting into any receptacle provided for the purpose or into any drain.

28(b) Any person pretending or professing to tell fortunes, or using any subtle craft, means, or device, by palmistry or otherwise, to deceive and impose upon any person shall be deemed to be a rogue and vagabond and shall be liable to a fine not exceeding 250 ringgit or to imprisonment for a term not exceeding six months or to both.

Source: Minor Offences Act 1955

SOME BIZARRE MALAYSIAN SOUPS

Gearbox soup
Made from the bones of a cow or sheep, this soup is boiled for many hours, seasoned with local herbs and spices, and served hot over a bed of noodles. A large straw accompanies the soup to enable diners to suck the marrow out of the bones.

Torpedo soup
The penis of a bull is the main ingredient of this spicy soup, which is reputed to be an aphrodisiac. Costing up to RM15 per bowl, torpedo soup is among the most expensive street foods in the country.

SOME NOTORIOUS MALAYSIAN MURDERS

Date	Description of the victims and crime	Final outcome
2017	**Kim Jong-nam**, the half-brother of North Korean leader Kim Jong-un, and the oldest son of former North Korean leader Kim Jong-il, is attacked with VX nerve gas in Terminal 2 of Kuala Lumpur International Airport.	Two women were arrested with both claiming they had no idea that what they used as nerve gas, with one convicted of 'voluntarily causing injuries by dangerous weapons or means' and jailed for three years and four months.
2015	Deputy Public Prosecutor **Anthony Kevin Morais** is abducted on his way to work, his body found twelve days later.	Six men are found guilty of murder and sentenced to death.
2013	A Bahraini banker, Hussain Najadi, 75, based in Kuala Lumpur, is shot dead after leaving the Guan Yin Temple in Kuala Lumpur.	A 'hitman', Koong Swee Kwan is later convicted for the 'contract killing' and is sentenced to death.
2007	Noor Azura Mohd-Yusoff, a 22-year-old Malaysian prostitute, was charged in London along with her Vietnamese boyfriend with the murder of Chinese national **Xie Xing Xing**, whose headless body was found floating in a marina in South London.	Noor Azura was convicted of Xie's murder and sentenced to life in prison in England. Her boyfriend was convicted of perverting justice by disposing of the body in the River Thames.
2007	The body of Singaporean **Goh Yoke Seng**, chopped into 11 pieces in black rubbish bags, was found in a refrigerator in Kuala Lumpur. The new owner of a luxury condominium had noticed a foul smell before making the grizzly discovery. The murder allegedly took place two years prior to the discovery of the body.	Goh's wife, Nora Jawi, was suspected of the crime and arrested. She was later released due to lack of evidence. The case remains unsolved.
2006	A Mongolian, Shaariibuugiin Altantuyaa, is found dead in Shah Alam, either killed in an explosion, of murdered before the explosion.	Chief Inspector Azilah Hadri and Corporal Sirul Azhar Umar, were found guilty and sentenced to death. Acquitted by the Court of Appeal, the latter fled to Australia, with the Federal Court subsequently overturning the appeal court decision.

Date	Description of the victims and crime	Final outcome
2003	Hanif Basree Abdul Rahman, a 40-year-old Shah Alam City Council engineer, was charged with murdering 22-year-old part-time guest relations officer **Noritta Samsudin**. The victim's naked body was found in her apartment in Sri Hartamas.	Hanif Basree was acquitted in July 2004. The prosecution appealed this decision, but the Federal Court dismissed the case in 2008.
2003	Aircraft cabin cleaner Ahmad Najib Aris was charged with raping and murdering IT Analyst **Canny Ong**, who was abducted in a car park in Bangsar. Her charred remains were found at a construction site off Old Klang Road in Kuala Lumpur.	Ahmad Najib was sentenced to death for the murder in 2005 and was executed in 2016.
2000	Kenneth Lee Fook Mun, grandson of the first Finance Minister Tun Sir H.S. Lee, was charged with the murder of accountant **Lee Good Yew** killed during Kenneth's shooting spree on Jalan Bukit Petaling, Kuala Lumpur.	Convicted of murder and sentenced to death in 2006, Kenneth Lee's death sentence was commuted to life imprisonment in 2008.
1993	*Bomoh* (traditional Malay healer) Mohd Affandi Abdul Rahman, his wife, Mona Fandey, and their assistant were charged with murdering Batu Talam State Assemblyman **Datuk Mazlan Idris**, who had sought the *bomoh*'s assistance to oust his political rivals. The victim's body was found, beheaded and chopped up, buried in a storeroom near Mona's house.	The body of Batu Talam State Assemblyman Datuk Mazlan Idris was found, beheaded and chopped up, buried in a storeroom near the home of Mona Fandey, wife of *Bomoh* (traditional Malay healer) Mohd Affandi Abdul Rahman; Mazlan Idris having sought the bomoh's assistance to oust political rivals.
1982	Culture, Youth and Sports Minister Datuk Mokhtar Hashim and Rahmat Satiman were charged with shooting former state Assemblyman **Taha Talib** outside his house.	Both perpetrators were sentenced to death. Datuk Mokhtar had his sentence commuted to life in 1984 and received a royal pardon in 1991. Rahmat Satiman appealed his conviction and was released in 1983.
1980	Lecturer S. Karthigesu was charged with killing his former sister-in-law, beauty queen **Jean Sinappa**, in a crime of passion and jealousy.	Karthigesu was found guilty and sentenced to death. His conviction was overturned and he was freed after a key prosecution witness admitted giving false evidence.

Height in metres of the National Monument in Kuala Lumpur:

Date	Description of the victims and crime	Final outcome
1975	The Chief Police Officer of Perak, **Tan Sri Koo Chong Kong**, and his Constable, **Yeong Peng Cheong**, were shot dead by two gunmen at a road junction. Communists Lim Woon Chong and Ng Foo Nam were charged with the murders in 1977.	In 1978, Lim and Ng were convicted of the murders and sentenced to death.
1974	Inspector General of Police **Tan Sri Abdul Rahman Hashim** was shot dead in his Mercedes by two gunmen at a junction on Jalan Tun Perak in Kuala Lumpur.	The perpetrators of the crime remain unknown.

THE FIRST SIKHS

Captain Tristram Speedy, the acting British Resident for Perak, was responsible for bringing the first group of 110 Sikhs to Malaya in 1873.

Source: *New Straits Times*
Note: This excludes Sikhs serving in the British/Indian armed forces.

GUIDELINES FOR MUSLIM ASTRONAUTS

Excerpts taken verbatim from the *Guidelines for Performing Islamic Rites at the International Space Station (ISS)*, a reference for Muslim astronauts written by the Department of Islamic Development Malaysia (JAKIM).

Determining the direction of qiblat
The direction of the qiblat shall be determined as much as possible in the following order:

a. Kaabah

b. Kaabah's projection

c. Earth

d. Any direction

Determining the prayer time
The time of the daily five prayers is defined within a 24 hour period (1 day on Earth) and shall follow the prayer times of the astronaut's point of departure.

Performing the fast
a. Fasting can be performed at the ISS... by way of qadha' (compensating for the missed fasting) where the month of Ramadhan is involved.
b. Fasting time shall follow the fasting time of the astronaut's point of departure.

Praying
The fundamental physical actions of the prayer are to be performed by the astronaut as the situation at the ISS permits, according the following order:
a. Upright standing. If he/she is unable to stand upright, then any standing position.
b. If the person is unable to stand up, then he/she may sit down. The ruku' (bowing) may be performed by bending the head so that it is parallel to the knees or even better, parallel to the place of prostration.
c. If the person is unable to sit, he/she may lie down on his/her right side facing the qiblat.
d. If the person is unable to lie down on his/her right side, he/she may lie down on his/her back.
e. If the person is unable to lie down on his/her back, he/she may perform the fundamental physical actions of the prayer by gesturing with the eyelids for each prayer movement.
f. If the person is still unable to do the above, then he/she shall pass the actions of the prayer through his/her mind, i.e. by imagining himself/herself standing, bowing, prostrating, etc.

Managing the dead
a. The dead body must be returned to Earth so that it can be managed as usual.
b. If the dead body cannot be returned to Earth, then it is permissible to lay it to rest in space by performing a simple funeral ceremony.

Food
If there is any doubt on the halal status of the food prepared, it may be consumed to alleviate hunger only.

Etiquette of travelling
a. The journey to space is a journey which is permissible in Islam.
b. Astronauts must observe the etiquettes of travelling:
   – Maintaining relationship with God.
   – Maintaining harmonious relationships among people.
   – Preserving the space environment.

20 RICHEST MALAYSIANS IN 2022

Name Net Worth (USD)	Age	Family	Main Companies
1. **Robert Kuok** $11 billion	99	married, 8 children	Kuok Group, Wilmar International
2. **Quek Leng Chan** $10 billion	80	married, 3 children	Hong Leong Group
3. **Koon Poh Keong** **(and siblings)** $6.2 billion	61	married	Press Metal
4. **Teh Hong Piow** $5.7 billion	92	married, 4 children	Public Bank
5. **Ananda Krishnan** $5 billion	84	married, 3 children	PanOcean Management
6. **Lee Yeow Chor** **(and Lee Yeow Seng)** $4.8 billion	56	married	IOI Group
7. **Chen Lip Keong** $2.7 billion	74	married, 3 sons	NagaCorp
8. **Tan Yu Yeh and Tan Yu Wei** $2.4 billion	51	--	D.I.Y
9. **Lim Kok Thay** $2.35 billion	71	married, 3 children	Genting Group
10. **Lau Cho Kun** $2 billion	86	married, 1 child	Hap Seng Consolidated
11. **Kuan Kam Ho** **(and family)** $1.9 billion	75	married	Hartalega Holdings
12. **Lee Oi Hian** **(and Hau Hian)** $1.6 billion	71	married, 4 children	Batu Kawan, Kuala Lumpur Kepong
13. **G. Gnanalingam** $1.55 billion	79	married, 3 children	Westports Malaysia

14. **Lim Wee Chai** $1.4 billion	64	married	Top Glove
15. **Syed Mokhtar AlBukhary** $1.31 billion	70	married, 5 children	Albukhary Group
16. **Jeffrey Cheah** $1.3 billion	76	married, 3 children	Sunway Group
17. **Francis Yeoh** (and siblings) $1.2 billion	68	widowed, 5 children	YTL Corporation
18. **Surin Upatkoon** $1.05 billion	71	married, 3 children	Intouch Holdings
19. **Tiong Hiew King** (and family) $1 billion	87	married	Rimbunan Hijau
20. **Ninian Mogan Lourdenadin** $960 million	68	married, 4 children	MBF Holdings

Source: Forbes

ORIGINS OF THE SPIRIT BADI GAJAH

According to one of the many spirit stories of the Mah Meri Orang Asli tribe, there was an old woman who became deaf because caterpillars had entered her ears. People did not like her because she was deaf. The woman had become stupid because the caterpillars had eaten up her brain. One night she had a dream and in that dream she was told to look for an elephant's trunk.

She was afraid to do so, as the elephant was big and she was only a woman. Nevertheless, she found the elephant and cut off its trunk and ran away with it, leaving the elephant struggling and screaming.

When she was far away, she was at ease and wanted to sleep, but found that she had no pillow. So she had to use the elephant's trunk. When she was fast asleep, the smell of the elephant's blood from the trunk made the caterpillars come out from her ears and she was able to hear again. But her skull was empty. When she died, she became the spirit Badi Gajah.

Source: *Mah-Meri* by Roland Werner, 1997

FOREIGNERS WHO WENT MISSING IN MALAYSIA

Description of missing person	Circumstances of disappearance	Theories about disappearance
Jim Thompson, an American businessman, helped revitalise the Thai silk and textile industry in the 1950s and 1960s. Thompson served as a US intelligence officer in Europe and Asia during World War II. After the war, he moved to Thailand and started the successful Jim Thompson Thai Silk Company. Many, however, suspected that he was still covertly involved in intelligence activities.	Thompson disappeared while on an Easter Sunday walk in Cameron Highlands in Pahang at 3 p.m. on 26 March 1967. He was on vacation with friends, staying at the Moonlight Cottage. He went for a walk in the jungle alone without telling anybody, leaving behind his suit jacket, cigarettes, lighter and the pills that he had been taking to relieve gallstone pains. This suggests that he didn't plan on being gone very long.	Numerous theories have been put forth: he died accidentally in the jungle as a result of disorientation, an animal trap, or a sudden health problem; he was kidnapped for ransom or political purposes; or he committed suicide. None of these theories, however, has been proven.
Bruno Manser, a Swiss environmental activist, took a deep interest in rainforest preservation and the protection of indigenous peoples in Sarawak. From 1984 to 1990, he lived among the nomadic Penan people of Sarawak. Manser fought vociferously against the timber operators in Sarawak, whom he believed were destroying the natural environment. He was consequently deported from Sarawak and barred from returning. However, he illegally entered Sarawak in early 2000 to rejoin his Penan friends.	Manser was last seen in May 2000 with members of the Penan tribe in an isolated village in the Kelabit Highlands of Sarawak. A letter which he sent to his girlfriend on 22 May 2000 is his last known correspondence. His whereabouts remain unknown.	Among the numerous theories which have been suggested, the most credible possibilities are that Manser got lost in the rainforest and met with an accidental death, that he was a victim of foul play or that he is presently living somewhere deep in the jungle among the Penan community.

Description of missing person	Circumstances of disappearance	Theories about disappearance
George Laub, a Danish chemical engineer working in Muar, was a major in Johore Volunteer Force.	In late November he left Malaya for Thailand to check what preparations the Japanese were making for invasion.	He was last seen alive by his colleagues on 1 December 1941 in the Malayan-Thai border region and may have been killed that day by Japanese agents, or on 13 December 1941, or at some later date.

A LETTER TO THE RANEE OF SARAWAK, 1920

Madam,

I am immensely gratified and touched by the letter you have been good enough to write to me. The first Rajah Brooke has been one of my boyish admirations, a feeling I have kept to this day strengthened by the better understanding of the greatness of his character and the unstained rectitude of his purpose. The book [Lord Jim] which has found favour in your eyes has been inspired in great measure by the history of the first Rajah's enterprise and even by the lecture of his journals...

It was never my good fortune to see Kuching, and indeed my time in the Archipelago was short, though it left the most vivid impressions and some highly valued memories.

I beg to subscribe myself your Highness's most faithful and humble servant.

Joseph Conrad

EXECUTION BY KRIS

Before the 19th century, the sultans of the Malay Peninsula would order some executions to be carried out using the kris. The executioner would stand with a long kris behind the condemned man. A small piece of cotton wool was placed on the shoulder of the condemned man to staunch the bleeding. The executioner would hold the blade of the kris perpendicularly and then drive it down through the collarbone into the condemned man's heart. Death was almost instantaneous. The cotton wool was held in place as the blade was withdrawn.

AN ORANG ASLI ANIMAL LEGEND

Once upon a time, the moonrat was the king of all of the animals of the forest. He was incredibly ugly, with a long pig-like snout, webbed duck-like feet and coarse, shaggy black hair on his back. As a king, the moonrat was a cruel and ruthless tyrant.

One day, the moonrat decided that he wanted to cut down a huge tree in order to build a boat and see the world. The other animals dutifully built him a big, beautiful boat, but when it was finished the moonrat declared that it was too big and ordered them to make it smaller. But even after this was done, the moonrat was still not satisfied and ordered the other animals to make it smaller. This continued until only a splinter of wood remained, and the moonrat picked up the splinter and began to pick his teeth with it.

Exhausted and angered, the other animals demanded an explanation from the moonrat. He replied that, as their king, if he didn't keep them busy they would rebel against him. This comment further enraged the other animals and they turned against the moonrat, seizing him and belching and vomiting on his body, and finally chasing him away into the forest.

Ever since then the moonrat, ashamed to show himself in public, moves about only in the moonlight. But one can always tell when he is coming by the strong, putrid stench that he emits.

Source: *Orang Asli Animal Tales* by Lim Boo Liat, 1981

THE LEANING TOWER OF MALAYSIA

Constructed in 1885 and initially used as a water storage tower, the Leaning Tower of Teluk Intan started to tilt four years after its construction owing to a flood from the Perak River.

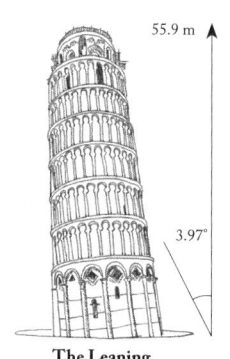

The Leaning Tower of Pisa

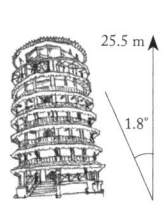

The Leaning Tower of Teluk Intan

THINGS FOUND ON THE LRT AND BUSES (JANUARY 2008–APRIL 2009)

Item	Number
Wallets	15
Keys, including car keys	6
Office identification cards/tags	5
Insurance/medical cards	3
ATM cards	3
Driver's licences	3
Touch 'n Go cards	3
Documents	3
Loyalty cards	3
Bags	3
University/college cards	2
Files	2
Road tax stickers	2
Other cards	2
Watches	2
Identity cards	1
Neckties	1
Slippers	1
Mobile phones	1
Cash	1 (RM11)
Total	**62**

Source: Ebi Azly Abdullah, General Manager of Communications, RapidKL

NUMBER OF REGISTERED MARRIAGES AND DIVORCES, 2020

	Marriages	Divorces
Muslim	145,202	37,853
Non-Muslim	38,387	7,901

Source: Department of Statistics Malaysia

Age of Prime Minister Dato' Sri Najib Tun Razak when he was elected Member of Parliament for Pekan in 1976:

THE OLDEST EXISTING MEMBERS' CLUBS

Club	Year established	Current location	Present total number of members
Penang Turf Club	1864	Penang	500+
Penang Club	1868	Georgetown, Penang	2,600
Malacca Club	c. 1880	Melaka	unknown
Royal Selangor Club	1884	Merdeka Square, Kuala Lumpur	6,500+
Perak Turf Club	1886	Ipoh, Perak	apx. 400
Royal Sungei Ujong Club	1887	Seremban, Negeri Sembilan	apx. 1,400
Royal Lake Club	1890	Lake Gardens, Kuala Lumpur	8,900+
New Taiping Club	1892	Taiping	998
Royal Ipoh Club	c. 1895	Ipoh, Perak	apx. 1,300
Selangor Turf Club	1896	Sungai Besi, Selangor	670
Penang Sports Club (formed as the Penang Cricket Club)	1900	Jalan Utama, Penang	3,700
Royal Klang Club	1901	Klang, Selangor	apx. 1,300
Penang Swimming Club	1903	Tanjung Bungah, Penang	apx. 6,500
Royal Kedah Club	1909	Alor Star, Kedah	1,360
Gymkhana Club	1913	Miri, Sarawak	660
Lower Perak Club	1932	Teluk Intan, Perak	380

THIS MAY HURT A LITTLE BIT

Traditional method of tattooing by the Kayan tribe of Sarawak:
- Wait until just after the harvest, when there is little work to be done in the fields.
- Pay the tattoo artist before she begins her work.
- Say a prayer to request for a minimal amount of pain and good work on the part of the tattoo artist.
- Using wooden blocks with designs carved into them, the tattoo artist will print the pattern of the tattoo in ink (made from scorched damar, sugarcane juice and water) on the arm, hand, leg or foot.
- The tattoo artist will dip the head of a hammer-like implement (with two or three needles protruding from it) into the ink.
- By hitting the end of the hammer-like implement with a stick, the tattoo artist will drive the tattoo into the skin.
- Keep the tattoo uncovered and dry for two weeks, and occasionally apply a cold sugar-water solution to bring out a bluer hue.

MALAYA'S MOST WANTED

The following monetary awards, in Straits dollars, were offered in the early 1950s by the British colonial authorities for providing information leading to the apprehension of Communist Party of Malaya members.

Secretary-General of the Central Executive Committee	$250,000
Members of the Politburo	$25,000
Members of the Malayan Bureau	$20,000
State Committee Secretaries	$15,000
State Committee Members	$10,000
District Committee Secretaries	$7,000
District Committee Members	$5,000
Members of Platoon Commands	$3,000
Members of Branch Committees	$2,500
Leaders of Party Cells	$1,500
Ordinary Party Members	$1,000

Source: *My Side of History* by Chin Peng, 2003

GUIDELINES ON NAMING CHILDREN

The Malaysian National Registration Department prohibits parents from giving their children the following types of names, which are deemed to be undesirable and objectionable:

- **Royal or ancestral titles** such as Syarifah, Syed, Tunku, Tengku, Raja
- **Titles awarded by the Malaysian Royalty** such as Tun, Tan Sri, Dato', Datin, Puan Seri, Dato' Patinggi
- **Names denoting positions** such as Haji, Nabi (prophet), Ketua Menteri (Chief Minister), Perdana Menteri (Prime Minister), Queen, King, Hakim (judge)
- **Professional names** such as Dr (doctor), Ir (engineer), Professor, Akauntan (accountant), Auditer (auditor), Diplomat
- **Warrior or other titles** such as Mahaguru (Grand Master), Pahlawan (warrior), Satria (warrior/knight), Bomoh (medicine man/shaman)
- **Lewd names** such as Bontot (buttocks), Zina (adultery), Khalwat (close proximity), Coli (brassiere), Liwat (sodomy)
- **Names with negative connotations** such as Buruk (bad/ugly), Sial (bad luck), Derita (suffering), Hapak (stale), Baruah (minion)
- **Names of accessories or attire** such as Cincin (ring), Subang (earring), Benang (thread), Kain (cloth), Kasut (shoes)
- **Arabic names with unpleasant meanings** such as Narul (hell), Zani (adulterer), Zaniah (adulteress), Khinzir (swine), Woti (sexual intercourse)
- **Names of insects or animals** such as Babi (pig), Keldai (donkey), Rimau (tiger)
- **Names of fruits, vegetables, plants or food** such as Ciku, Keladi (yam), Serai (lemongrass), Bubur (porridge), Daun (leaf)
- **Peculiar names** such as Kecut (shrink), Kuyok (command to call a dog), Boyak (fat and potbellied), Kudung (cripple), Pendek (short), Apek (old Chinese man), Ketiak (underarm), Leper, Kemek (flat), Tanduk (horns), Kerepot (shrivelled)
- **Names of natural phenomena** such as Salji (snow), Suria (sun), Awan (clouds), Bulan (moon), Bumi (earth), Angkasa (heavens)
- **Names of household items** such as Senduk (ladle), Mangkuk (bowl), Tilam (mattress), Berus (brush), Garfu (fork)
- **Names of colours** such as Putih (white), Merah (red), Coklat (brown)
- **Names comprising letters of the alphabet or numbers or a combination of both** such as D, K, 001, 007 or Zero-zero Seven, K.7, K.4

- **Indian names with strange or unpleasant meanings** such as Karuppusamy (black man), Kulli (pothole/coolie), Nondy (cripple), Peyan (devil), Pitchai (beggar), Madayan (idiot), Paraiandy (pariah), Kakayan (crow), Mottayan (bald), Pooci (insect)
- **Chinese names with strange or unpleasant meanings** in Hokkien, Cantonese, and Mandarin such as Khwye Chiew/Pai Sau/Why So (cripple), Ah Sai/Ar See (faeces), Chow Kow/Schow Khow (smelly dog), Chow Lok/Chang Chee (whore)

A SELECTION OF "THE WORST"

Event	Date and Place	Description
The worst fire	1989, Guar Chempedak, Kedah	27 girls killed when the Taufiqiah Al-Khairiah madrasa caught fire during the night.
The worst landslide	1993, Ulu Klang, Selangor	48 people were killed when a block of the Highland Towers collapsed
The worst haze	2005, Port Klang, Selangor	Officials declared a state of emergency after the Air Pollutant Index breached the hazardous 500 mark
The worst road accident	2013, Genting Highlands	The driver and 36 passengers were killed when the bus they were in plunged into a deep ravine
The worst blackout	1996, Peninsular Malaysia	Peninsular Malaysia was plunged into darkness when the national power grid collapsed
The worst train accident	1972, Kota Bharu, Kelantan	10 people died when two trains collided
The worst flood	1971, Peninsular Malaysia	22 people died and thousands were displaced when non-stop torrential rains caused massive flooding
The worst tsunami	2004, Langkawi and Penang	66 people were reported dead when the tsunami hit the northern coast of Malaysia
The worst tropical cyclone	1996, Peninsular Malaysia	Tropical Storm Greg hits Malaysia with 238 confirmed killed, and 102 missing, presumed killed
The worst airplane crash*	1977, Johor Bahru, Johor	100 people were killed when a Malaysia Airlines jetliner was hijacked and crashed

*This excludes the disappearance of MH370 on 8 March 2014 and the shooting down of MH17 over Ukraine on 17 July 2014.

MALAYSIA'S 10 MOST VALUABLE BRANDS, 2021

Brand	Industry	Brand value (US dollars)
1. Petronas	Energy	$12,049 million
2. Maybank	Banking	$3,661 million
3. Genting	Leisure/Entertainment	$3,130 million
4. Tenaga Nasional	Energy	$2,623 million
5. Sime Darby	Property/Infrastructure	$2,103 million
6. Public Bank	Banking	$1,753 million
7. CIMB	Banking	$1,734 million
8. Maxis	Communications	$1,552 million
9. Airasia	Airlines	$1,222 million
10. DiGi	Telecoms	$1,012 million

Source: Statista

HOW TO MAKE TUAK

Tuak is an alcoholic beverage made of fermented rice. It is a traditional drink of the Iban community in Sarawak, especially during the Gawai Festival every year.

1. Cook 5 kg of **glutinous rice**.
2. Cool rice in a flat utensil.
3. Pound 5 kg of round **ragi** (**yeast**) and 5 pieces of thinly sliced ragi into powder.
4. Mix ragi into cooled rice.
5. Ferment mixture in clean container for a week.
6. Pour **sugar syrup** to taste and **cold water** into mixture.
7. Ferment mixture for another week, for maximum effect. Alcohol content may vary from 10% to 50%, depending on the duration of fermentation.

HOW TO CATCH A HERD OF ELEPHANTS

Adapted from the *Hikayat Abdullah*, the 19th-century autobiography of Munshi Abdullah bin Abdul Kadir, a famous Malay scholar and teacher.

1. Cut giant poles—as thick as a man's thigh and 20 feet long—from jungle trees.
2. Drive the poles into the ground six inches apart and tie them tightly together with rope, making an enclosure measuring about 120 feet square.
3. On top of this barrier, build a wooden platform where people can stand.
4. Place sugar cane stems and banana trees along a path leading to the enclosure.
5. Go into the jungle, locate a herd of elephants, and drive them out by firing guns and yelling.
6. The elephants, tempted by the sugar cane and bananas along the path, will consume the foods and will be led docilely into the enclosure.
7. After the elephants enter the enclosure, barricade the entrance.
8. Prod the elephants with sticks and swords when they try to break down the fence of the enclosure.
9. Keep the elephants in the enclosure for 10 days without food or water.
10. Lower rattan nooses, baited with bananas, into the enclosure. Pull them tight around the elephants' necks and tie the other ends to trees.
11. Go inside the enclosure and fix chains to the elephants' flanks. Lead them out of the enclosure.
12. Avoid giving the elephants food or water, as they are much easier to handle in a weakened condition and should only be fed when their behaviour merits it.

NOT JUST A HOLE IN THE WALL

The Sarawak chamber in the Lubang Nasib Bagus cave in the Mulu National Park in Sarawak is the largest cavern in the world—700 metres long, with an average width of 300 metres (at its widest 396 metres), and a height of 70 metres. That is big enough to accommodate 40 Boeing 747s, stacked, or 10 Jumbos parked nose-to-nose. Alternatively, it could accommodate St Peter's Basilica in Rome.

BIDAYUH HEADHUNTING SONGS

Translation of a traditional prayer sung by male members of the Bidayuh tribe of Sarawak before they embarked on a headhunting expedition:

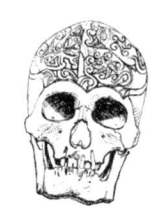

A normal character in ordinary time,
He can make himself a brave fighter,
And a hero when the time comes for revenge against his enemies.
We have kept the skulls for too long,
It is now time to go and get new ones.
Now we are on a headhunting expedition,
Let us say farewell to the spirits of our ancestors,
Let us give them the gifts of these rice grains,
And the heads of the beheaded enemies.

Translation of a traditional song sung to those male members of the Bidayuh tribe who did not wish to join a headhunting expedition:

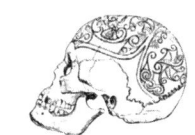

It is a pity you do not join us in the headhunting venture,
But all you can do is look after the baruk*.
You are not brave enough,
You have no idea what the spirits of our ancestors told us,
This is because you did not join us in the katang*.
As you had joined me in this successful headhunting expedition,
I gave you the chin part of the skull for you to show to your people.
But as the dog had grabbed it from your hand, you had nothing to show.
Because you are a drunkard
You never realised
That your wife
Was having an affair with another man.

* *baruk*–traditional structure used for ceremonial gatherings and for the storage of skulls.
* *katang*–a ceremony to appease the spirits of people who were headhunted.

TRADITIONAL MALAY METHOD TO MAKE A TOAD CRAZY AND BITE SOMEONE'S ARMPIT

- Mix and grind datura and opium seeds together.
- Feed the ingredients to a large red toad and spread them on its face.
- Set the toad free near the house of the intended victim.

Source: *Royal Healer* by Roland Werner, 2002
Note: The possession and use of opium are strictly prohibited under Malaysian law. (See p. 130)

FROM THE MALAYAN SONGBOOK

A selection of lyrics from the early 1960s book entitled *700 Most Popular Songs*:

"Around the Corner and Under the Tree"

Around the corner and under the tree
A Bengali Lady made love to me.
She said to me: "Mana pergi?"
And ever since that blinking day
I took minyak-sapi.

Around the corner and under the tree
A Tamil Lady made love to me.
She said to me: "Enga porah?"
And ever since that blinking day
I took ka-tri-ka ca-dra-va-ra.

Around the corner and under the tree
A Malay Lady made love to me.
She said to me: "Apa macham?"
And ever since that blinking day
I took sambal-blachan.

Around the corner and under the tree
A Chinese Lady made love to me.
She said to me: "Lu-khi-ta-lok?"
And ever since that blinking day
I took "Chin-cha-loh".

"Island of Penang"

O island of Penang humble pearl of the orient
With thy shores graced with swaying palms
And the sparkling sea beneath the tropical sun.

This is my island, my native home
My dearest thought wherever I roam
I may be parted many a seas
But my heart will be left in thee.

I see women on bended knees
Planting rice for her family
And running along the water side
Casting nets at the surging tide.

Tapping from the morn of the day
Our rubber tappers quiet and gay
For when they start at 5 o'clock
No tigers taking their morning walk.

As shadows lengthen in setting sun
Men hasten home as the day is done
As night slowly comes to rule
As night slowly comes to rule
Many go out to have a rendezvous.

HOW TO STRETCH THE EARLOBES, ORANG ULU STYLE

1. When a child is six months old, perforate his or her earlobes and insert heavy brass or copper rings or ornaments.
2. Gradually add more, heavier rings or ornaments, increasing the weight on the earlobes and thereby causing them to strain and split.
3. When the earlobes reach the desired length, he or she may want to remove the rings and ornaments to prevent further stretching.

BENTONG KALI: PROFILE OF AN INFAMOUS MALAYSIAN GANGSTER

1961	Born on 22 January in Bentong, Pahang and named after the Hindu goddess of destruction, Kaliamma.
1975	At the age of 14, he dropped out of school and joined a Chinese gang called "04".
1979–80	Released from prison at the age of 18, married at 19.
c. 1980	Moved to Kuala Lumpur and joined an Indian gang called "08". Also worked as a car repossessor.
1985	Arrested and sent to Pulau Jerejak near Penang. Released in 1987 and sent to Kuantan as a restricted resident.
1988	Returned to Kuala Lumpur and worked as a store detective for a department store.
1989	Formed his own gang, "04", and focused on distributing heroin in the Kuala Lumpur area.
1990	Arrested in a drug raid and sent to a restricted residence in Perak for two years.
1991	Escaped from custody and began a ruthless killing spree, eliminating drug and crime lords and anybody else who stood in his way.
1991	The police offered a RM100,000 for information leading to his arrest. In response, Bentong Kali personally telephoned CID Director Zaman Khan and dared him to try to arrest him.
c. 1991	Killed a total stranger after the victim scolded him for urinating in front of his flat.
1993	One hour after murdering his 17th victim, a *teh tarik* stall owner, Bentong Kali was shot dead by police after a raid on a terraced house in Medan Damansara. He was identified by the tattoos on his body of a dragon, tiger, nude women and the words "Born to Dai" (sic).

Source: Adapted from *Insider's Kuala Lumpur* by Lam Seng Fatt, 2004

WOVEN SYMBOLS ON SARAWAK BASKETS

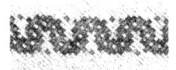
Creeper

Bamboo shoots

Leeches

Durian flowers

Birds

CHARM FOR THOSE WHO SWALLOWED A FISH BONE

Traditionally, the following prayer was repeated seven times by Malays and breathed over both eyes of the patient.

EATING ADVICE FROM THE ILLUSTRATED GUIDE TO THE FEDERATED MALAY STATES, 1923

"Food in Malaya consists of very much the same dishes as those obtainable in the Western civilised World, but there are a few things which are best avoided altogether. Of these uncooked vegetables are the most to be shunned. That delight in warm climates—the salad, in all its forms—is dangerous in the East for you cannot be certain whether the water which washed it was pure or the methods of the grower entirely beyond sanitary suspicion. Another frequent cause of offendings is the Malay curry eaten without understanding. This dish, for those who like spiced meats, is a joy, but like other violent delights it is apt to have violent ends, and it should be eaten with strict moderation. Particularly one should shun the little dried prawns which appear so innocently amongst the sambals or little side dishes which accompany the main dish of curried fowl. They have been known to set up a poisoning which may be ptomaine or may be merely a form of shell-fish poisoning, but whatever it be it is exceedingly painful, often dangerous, and has been before now fatal. Surfeits of tropical fruits may be responsible for much discomfort. Milk unboiled is, for a certainty, mixed with water, and the water, for a probability, mixed with typhoid. Water is safe enough usually if it comes from a pipe supply, but in no country is unboiled water above suspicion, and it is not recommended as a beverage in Malaya."

MOBILE MEALS

Roti man
The *roti* (bread) man visits certain residential areas in Kuala Lumpur every evening on his *kapcai* (motorcycle). Affixed to the back of his vehicle is a large metal container, in which he keeps all sorts of breads and buns. Snacks, crisps and chocolates are usually stored in clear plastic bags strategically tied to the outside of the metal box, in clear view of children.

Tau foo far man
Tau foo far is essentially curdled soy milk that is a healthy Chinese dessert. It has a smooth, tofu-like consistency, and is usually served warm with sugar syrup or palm sugar (*gula melaka*). The *tau foo far* man typically drives a bike or van equipped with a metal container to keep the *tau foo far* warm. A separate container is used to keep the syrup or palm sugar, which is poured over the *tau foo far* before being served.

Cendol and rojak man
Rojak and *cendol*, two of Malaysia's most popular tea-time snacks, are usually sold together. The most important apparatus the seller has with him is an ice-shaving machine, used to make *cendol*, a dessert served with coconut milk and *gula melaka*. He also keeps the fried ingredients and peanut sauce that make up the *rojak*, a salad-like snack, in his bike or van.

Yong tau foo man
Yong tau foo is a Malaysian Hakka dish in which tofu and different types of vegetables, such as brinjal, okra, chilli and bitter gourd, are stuffed with fish paste and boiled in clear broth. The *yong tau foo* man usually drives a van in which he keeps a portable burner, a pot of boiling soup, a chopping board along with the vegetables and tofu. Buying a meal is as easy as walking up to the van with a dish or bowl and choosing from the array of vegetables and tofu.

Noodle man
As the name suggests, the noodle man sells different noodle dishes, from *kon low mee* (noodles mixed with dark soy sauce) to *mee* soup. Attached to the noodle man's motorcycle is a boiling pot of soup, which is used to heat up and soften the pre-cooked

noodles. Depending on the type of dish, different condiments—such as garlic oil, minced meat, onions, pork and fish balls—accompany the noodles.

Dim sum man
The *dim sum* man rides a motorcycle to which he ties a steamer (which also acts as a container) in which he keeps different light dishes—such as dumplings, fish and meat balls—that make up the *dim sum*. Although *dim sum* is a popular Chinese breakfast cuisine, the *dim sum* man sells the dishes all day long, even at night.

Market or vegetable man
These mobile grocers usually drive a lorry in which they store and display their products, ranging from fresh produce and meats to fish and tinned or bottled foods. They usually take the same route through residential areas at about the same time every day so their customers know when to expect them.

Pau man
Like the *roti* man, the *pau* (Chinese bread buns) man keeps his buns in a multi-tiered steamer attached to the back or side of his motorcycle. The steamed buns, which have different fillings, such as red-bean paste, *char siew* (barbequed pork) and lotus paste, are kept in separate tiers.

Ice cream man
A metal container is attached to the back of the ice cream man's motorcycle, just like that of the *roti* man. The box functions as a freezer in which he keeps the frozen treats. Instead of playing jingles over the loud speakers of the van, the ice cream seller on the motorbike usually sounds a horn or rings a bell tied to his vehicle.

Nasi kandar man
Nasi kandar, a popular local rice dish, is so called because of the method in which it used to be sold. Vendors would *kandar* (carry) and balance a pole on their shoulders. Tied to both ends of the pole were containers or baskets of rice meals. The *nasi* (rice) is accompanied by side dishes such as curry, fried chicken, brinjal, okra or bittergourd. The dish, however, is no longer sold in this method. Instead, one can enjoy *nasi kandar* at *mamak* restaurants around the country.

WHO IS A MALAY?

The Federal Constitution of Malaysia refers to a Malay as "a person who professes the religion of Islam, habitually speaks the Malay language, conforms to Malay custom and:

a. was before Merdeka Day born in the Federation or in Singapore or born of parents one of whom was born in the Federation or in Singapore, or is on that day domiciled in the Federation or in Singapore; or
b. is the issue of such a person."

Source: Laws of Malaysia: Federal Constitution (incorporating all amendments up to 1 January 2006)

CASUALTIES IN ROAD ACCIDENTS

Road accident figures

Year	Accidents	Fatalities
2010	414,421	6,872
2011	449,040	6,877
2012	462,426	6,917
2013	477,204	6.915
2014	476,196	6.674
2015	489,606	6,706
2016	521,466	7,152
2017	533,875	6,740
2018	548,598	6,284
2019	567,516	6,167

SCENTLESS FLOWER

The National Flower, the Chinese Hibiscus (*Hibiscus rosa-sinensis*, family Malvaceae), is an evergreen shrub native to East Asia. It has no scent.

PANTUN

Pantun (pronounced "pun-toon") are vehicles for the expression of poetic feelings, appearing as insets in Malay literature. *Pantun* are quatrains in which the first and third, and second and fourth, lines rhyme. They are a particularly effective form of expressing one's feelings about relationships, lessons learnt and love lost.

Illicit love

Kain ini kain sutera,   This waistcloth is silk so gay,
     Kalau mandi dibasah jangan.   That when you bathe you should not wet it.*
Main ini kita berdua,   This game's for two of us to play,
     Kalau mati menyesal jangan.   Should death result, do not regret it.

* Malays traditionally bathe in a washable cotton *sarong*. A silk *sarong* would be ruined in the process.

Bodily desire

Sakit kaki ditikam jeruju,   The prickles cause my feet to smart,
     Jeruju ada di dalam paya.   Sea-holly grows amidst the mire.
Sakit hati memandang susu,   The sight of breasts enflames my heart,
     Susu ada di dalam kebaya.   Beneath a woman's loose attire.*

* The *kebaya* is a traditional Peranakan costume for women.

KELANTANESE ADVICE FOR CHOOSING A BUILDING SITE

If one stays where the ground inclines from the **southeast**, one is bound to lose one's job or source of income.

If one stays where the ground inclines from the **south**, one is bound to suffer loss and death.

If one stays where the ground inclines from the **southwest**, one is bound to be envied by one's brothers and sisters and other relatives who are lazy, and as a result they will completely exhaust one's wealth.

If one stays where the ground inclines from due **west**, one is bound to become wild in one's ways and exhaust one's own wealth.

If one stays where the ground inclines from the **southwest**, one is bound to gain a new wife and a son who is extremely good.

It is best to stay where the ground inclines from the **northwest** towards the **east** and the **southwest**, for this is the prime location.

Source: *Royal Healer* by Roland Werner, 2002

STRUCTURE OF A TRADITIONAL MALAYSIAN CHINESE SECRET SOCIETY

General Headman
Oversees and directs a group of secret societies.

Master
Well-versed in the society's passwords, poems, rituals and legends. The master conducts initiation and other ceremonies.

District Headman
Issues orders and represents his society at all negotiations.

Judge
Mediates and settles disputes between societies.

Treasurer
Controls all of the society's funds. Often a legitimately employed, trustworthy businessman.

Coordinator
The leader of the Fighters. Ensures that newly initiated members are following the society's rules and regulations.

Fighters
Collect "subscription" fees within their own operational territory and guard against invasion from other societies.

Members
Known as *lao ma* (old horses) or *hsin ma* (new horses), the members obey orders from higher members of the society.

Source: *The Impact of Chinese Secret Societies in Malaya* by Wilfred Blythe, 1969

MALAYSIAN ARMED FORCES: PEACEKEEPING OPERATIONS

1960–1962	**United Nations Operation in Congo (UNOC)** Malaysian Armed Forces were dispatched as a part of a United Nations operation in the Congo.
1988–1991	**United Nations Iran–Iraq Military Observer Group (UNIIMOG)** Malaysian Armed Forces were dispatched as a part of a United Nations operation to supervise the Iran–Iraq War ceasefire.

1989–1990	**United Nations Transition Assistance Group (UNITAG)** Malaysian Armed Forces were dispatched as a part of a United Nations operation to supervise Namibia's elections and transition to independence.
1991–present	**United Nations Mission for the Referendum in Western Sahara (MINURSO)** Malaysian Armed Forces were dispatched as a part of a United Nations contingent to observe the implementation of a ceasefire between the Polisario Front and Morocco.
1991–1995	**United Nations Angola Verification Mission II (UNAVEM II)** Malaysian Armed Forces were dispatched as a part of a United Nations contingent to enforce a ceasefire in the civil war.
1992–2003	**United Nations Iraq–Kuwait Observation Mission (UNIKOM)** Malaysian Armed Forces were dispatched as a part of a United Nations contingent to monitor the demilitarised zone along the Iraq–Kuwait border.
1993–1995	**United Nations Operation in Somalia II (UNISOM II)** Malaysian Armed Forces were dispatched as a part of a United Nations contingent to take appropriate action to establish a secure environment for humanitarian assistance.
1993–1998	**United Nations Mission in Bosnia and Herzegovina (UNMIBH)** Malaysian Armed Forces were dispatched as a part of a United Nations contingent initially known as MALBATT (Malaysia Battalion) under the UN Protection Force. Later the Malaysian troops were redeployed as MALCON (Malaysia Contingent) Command under the NATO-led Implementation Force and Stabilisation Force.
1999-present	**United Nations Organization Stabilization Mission in the Democratic Republic of the Congo (MONUSCO)** Malaysia has contributed four experts and two soldiers.
2004–2008	**Southern Philippines** Troops were deployed as a part of a monitoring force agreed upon by both the Philippine Government and the Moro Islamic Liberation Front (MILF) to enforce a 2001 ceasefire agreement.
2006–2012	**United Nations Integrated Mission in Timor–Leste** Malaysian Armed Forces were dispatched as a part of a United Nations contingent to help quell escalating violence and unrest.
2007–present	**United Nations Interim Force in Lebanon** Malaysian Armed Forces were dispatched as a part of a United Nations operation to establish peace and security in Lebanon.
2011-present	**United Nations Mission in South Sudan (UNMISS)** Malaysia has contributed police to aid peacekeeping in South Sudan.

Source: Ministry of Defence Malaysia

BANNED MOVIES IN MALAYSIA

Under the Film Censorship Act 2002, the Film Censorship Board must view and approve every film before it is shown publicly in Malaysia. Films which contain objectionable ideological, political, religious, socio-cultural, sexual, violent or criminal elements are typically banned or censored. The following is a list of some of the films that have been banned in Malaysia over the years.

- A Clockwork Orange (1971)
- The Exorcist (1973)
- Saturday Night Fever (1977)
- Scarface (1983)
- Cannibal Holocaust (1984)
- Pet Sematary (1989)
- Schindler's List (1995)
- Babe (1995)
- Showgirls (1995)
- Last Man Standing (1996)
- Fire (1996)
- Orgazmo (1997)
- Boogie Nights (1997)
- Babe: Pig in the City (1998)
- The Prince of Egypt (1998)
- Austin Powers: The Spy Who Shagged Me (1999)
- South Park: Bigger, Longer & Uncut (1999)
- Dogma (1999)
- Eyes Wide Shut (1999)
- Fiza (2001)
- Zoolander (2001)
- Blade II (2002)
- Queen of the Damned (2002)
- 40 Days and 40 Nights (2002)
- Pinocchio (2002)
- Daredevil (2003)
- Kill Bill: Vol. 1 (2003)
- The Girl Next Door (2004)
- Sideways (2004)
- Harold & Kumar Go to White Castle (2004)
- The Passion of the Christ (2004) —shown only to Christian audiences
- Team America: World Police (2004)
- Alfie (2004)
- Deuce Bigalow: European Gigolo (2005)
- Sin City (2005)
- Hustle & Flow (2005)
- The 40-Year-Old Virgin (2005)
- Saw II (2005)
- Hard Candy (2005)
- Hostel (2005)
- Rent (2005)
- Brokeback Mountain (2005)
- Lelaki Komunis Terakhir (The Last Communist) (2006)
- See No Evil (2006)
- United 93 (2006)
- Saw III (2006)
- Borat (2006)
- Alpha Dog (2007)
- Hostel: Part II (2007)
- Halloween (2007)
- Saw IV (2007)
- I Don't Want to Sleep Alone (2007)
- Harold & Kumar Escape from Guantanamo Bay (2008)
- Step Brothers (2008)

- Pineapple Express (2008)
- Viswaroopam (2013)
- Dallas Byers Club (2013)
- The Wolf of Wall Street (2013)
- Noah (2015)
- The Danish Girl (2015)
- The Disaster Artist (2017)
- Padmaayat (2018)
- Babi (2020)
- The Battle of Lake Changin (2021)

Source: Internet Movie Database (IMDB)

WHAT WAS THERE BEFORE THEY WERE BUILT?

Now	Then
Istana Negara (1957)	Residence of millionaire Chan Wing
Menara Maybank (1987)	Sessions Court Building
Plaza Rakyat (under construction since 1992)	Selangor Chinese Club
Putrajaya (1995)	Harrisons & Crosfield Golden Hope Plantations
Mid Valley Megamall (1999)	Sri Maha Sakthi Muhambikai Amman Temple (subsequently rebuilt)
Petronas Twin Towers (1998)	Kuala Lumpur racecourse
Berjaya Times Square (2003)	Tycoon Cheong Yoke Choy's bungalow
Pavilion Kuala Lumpur (2007)	Bukit Bintang Girls' School

A BORNEO PYGMY ELEPHANT'S FAMILY RECIPE

Muddy Durian

Ingredients
- 1 durian
- Lots of mud

1. Roll the entire durian—spikes and all—in mud.
2. Swallow whole.

Borneo pygmy elephants also feed on palms, grass and wild bananas, consuming up to 150 kilograms of vegetation each day. Now found only in Sabah and East Kalimantan, Indonesia, their current population is estimated to be 1,500 or fewer.

Number of public holidays, including individual state holidays, celebrated in Malaysia annually:

SURVIVAL GUIDE: "HELP ME! I'VE BEEN BITTEN BY A..."

If you are bitten by any of the following poisonous animals in Malaysia, utter the following phrase:

"*Tolong! Saya disengat...* (insert name from list below)."

ampai-ampai . . . . stinging jelly fish	lintah . . . . water leech
halipan . . . . centipede	pachat . . . . jungle leech
ikan buntal . . . . puffer fish	penyengat . . . . hornet
ikan buntal pisang . . . . silvery puffer fish	semut api . . . . fire ant
ikan semaram . . . various scorpaenid fish	tebuan . . . . wasp
ikan sembilang . . . . catfish	ular kapak . . . . viper
ikan lepu . . . . scorpion fish	ular katam tebu . . . . krait
ikan pari . . . . stingray	ular laut . . . . sea snake
kala jengking . . . . small scorpion	ular mata hari . . . . coral snake
kerengga . . . . red ant	ular tedong abu . . . . king cobra
keroncho . . . . small king crab	ular tedong sendok . . . . cobra
belangkas . . . . large king crab	ular tuntong tebu . . . . banded sea snake
kumbang . . . . large wood-boring beetle	ulat . . . . worm, caterpillar
labah-labah . . . . spider	ulat bulu . . . . hairy caterpillar
lebah . . . . bee	ulat bulu laut . . . stinging marine worm

DOS AND DON'TS DURING THE HUNGRY GHOST FESTIVAL

During the Hungry Ghost Festival, which falls on the 7th month of the lunar calendar, the Chinese believe that the gates of hell are opened and the hungry ghosts of the deceased return to visit the living.

Do...

- leave an empty seat at your table and prepare sumptuous meals.
- burn candles, joss sticks, joss paper and fake paper money (called "Hell Money"), and other paper items including houses, transportation and accessories in front of your house.
- make food offerings (typically fruits such as rambutan, mangosteen and jackfruit as well as rice) in front of your house.

Don't...

- go swimming or jungle trekking.
- allow your children to wander the streets at night.
- move to a new home, start a new business or get married during this inauspicious period.
- enter a hotel room without knocking and asking for permission.
- sleep facing a mirror.

DEATH BY KNUCKLES

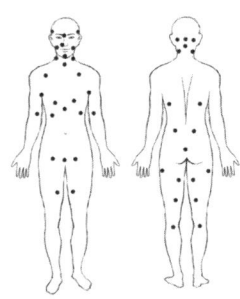

Seligi (knuckle) strikes are used in combat by silat exponents. Great care must be taken in executing these strikes which can rupture blood vessels and lead to extreme pain or even death. The diagram on the right shows the *seligi* target areas on the human body.

Source: *The Malay Art of Self-Defense* by Sheikh Shamsuddin, 2005.

THE FOUR ELEMENTS OF A HUMAN BEING

According to the Semai Orang Asli, human beings are made up of four elements:

> ***Kloog*** (heart soul)
> ***Ruwaay*** (head soul)
> ***Woog*** (shadow soul)
> ***Broog*** (body)

If the *kloog* leaves the *broog*, the person dies. The *ruwaay*, however, can leave the *broog* during a trance, sleep and unconsciousness. The *woog* is the supernatural partner of the *broog*.

HOW TO MAKE A SHADOW PUPPET OF SRI RAMA

1. Buy cow hide from a local butcher, remove all of the blood and fat from the inner side, stretch it on a wooden frame and put it out in the sun to dry for three days.
2. After the hide dries, scrape away the hair from its outer side. Soak the hide in water overnight, and use a brass-wire brush to scrape away any roughness.
3. Trace the outline of Sri Rama (the principal hero of the *Ramayana* epic) on a piece of white paper and cut it out. Using rice paste, stick the paper to the hide.
4. With a knife, cut out the figure from the hide. Use a chisel to cut out the intricate details of Sri Rama's costume and jewellery.
5. Attach a spine of wood or rattan along the back of the hide with a thread. A thinner wooden rod is fastened to the puppet's hand.
6. Paint Sri Rama's skin green and his costume and jewellery a variety of rich and vibrant colours.

Height in metres of the golden statue of Lord Murugan that stands in front of Batu Caves:

PROVERBIAL WISDOM

Malay	: *Rumah terbakar, tikus habis keluar.*
Literal translation	: The house was burnt, the rats escaped.
Meaning	: **The money was spent and nothing was attained.**

Malay	: *Tiada kepala ekor.*
Literal translation	: Without head or tail.
Meaning	: **Confusing or unintelligible.**

Malay	: *Layang-layang putus talinya.*
Literal translation	: A kite of which the cord is broken.
Meaning	: **At the mercy of fortune.**

Malay	: *Tepuk dada, tanya selera.*
Literal translation	: Pat your chest, ask what your appetite is like.
Meaning	: **Think first before you act.**

Malay	: *Naik kuda hijau.*
Literal translation	: To ride the green horse.
Meaning	: **To be intoxicated.**

Malay	: *Sudah diketahui daging haram, mengapa pula maka dimakan?*
Literal translation	: He knew it was forbidden meat, why then did he consume it?
Meaning	: **He knew she was betrothed to another, why then did he pursue her?**

Malay	: *Ada udang di sebalik batu.*
Literal translation	: A prawn behind a stone.
Meaning	: **A hidden agenda.**

Malay	: *Harapkan pagar, pagar makan padi.*
Literal translation	: Rely on the fence, the fence devours the rice crop.
Meaning	: **Being betrayed by someone you really trust.**

Malay	: *Kacang lupakan kulit.*
Literal translation	: The bean forgets its pod.
Meaning	: **A "nouveau riche" person who forgets his humble beginnings.**

Malay	: *Jatuh di atas tilam.*
Literal translation	: To fall on a mattress.
Meaning	: **To get a rich wife.**

Source: *The MBRAS book of 1,600 Malay Proverbs with Explanations in English,* Compiled by E.S. Hose, 1992

HOW TO TELL WHAT HAS BEEN RAIDING YOUR PANTRY

Maximum age of contestants on the Malaysian reality show Akademi Fantasia: 47

RITES OF PASSAGE: A REFERENCE FOR THE UNINITIATED

Event	When to visit	What to wear	What to bring	What to expect
Malay birth	Any time during the 44-day confinement period after birth.	Casual, but conservative, clothing.	Gifts for the newborn or cash in an envelope.	A short visit with the family and their newborn child at their house.
Malay marriage	During the final marital ceremony, called the *bersanding*, which is followed by a formal dinner.	Men should wear traditional Malay costume (*baju melayu*), *batik* or other formal wear. Women may wear traditional costumes or conservative outfits.	Gifts for the newlyweds' home or cash in an envelope.	The bridal couple will sit on a dais and the guests will approach and perform a series of rituals. Dinner will be served, accompanied by musical performances.
Malay death	As soon as possible after the death.	Black or white formal wear. Women should cover their heads with shawls.	Cash in an envelope.	A short visit with the bereaved family at their home and possibly an opportunity to view the body of the deceased.
Chinese birth	After the first 30 days of confinement, at the "full moon" ceremony.	Casual clothing. Avoid wearing black.	Gifts for the newborn, gold jewellery or cash in a red envelope.	A dinner at home or at a Chinese restaurant during which the newborn will make its first public appearance.
Chinese marriage	During the wedding dinner, which is held in the evening on the same day as the traditional tea ceremony.	Formal wear. Avoid wearing black.	Cash in a red envelope or gifts for the newlyweds. Do not give shoes, handkerchiefs or clocks.	A full course Chinese dinner at a hotel or restaurant, accompanied by karaoke and "*yam seng*" (bottoms up) drinking.

MALAYSIA AT RANDOM

Event	When to visit	What to wear	What to bring	What to expect
Chinese death	Before the burial (which occurs between three days and one week after the death), when the body of the deceased is kept in the family home.	Casual wear in sombre, muted colours such as grey, black, and white.	Cash in a white envelope.	A short visit with the bereaved family and an opportunity to pay your last respects. You will be given lighted joss sticks to hold while saying a prayer for the deceased.
Indian birth	Any time during the 30 to 41-day confinement period after birth. On the 16th day after birth, the name-giving ceremony is held.	Casual clothing	Gifts for the newborn, jewellery or cash in an envelope.	A short visit with the family and their newborn child. 31 days after the child's birth, both mother and child will undergo a purification rite.
Indian marriage	During the wedding ceremony, which is held in the temple hall. The wedding dinner is normally held at the bride's house, a hotel or a restaurant.	Formal wear or traditional Indian costume.	Gifts for the newlyweds' home or cash in an envelope.	The bridal couple, seated on a dais, will perform a series of rituals including the tying of the *thali* or sacred pendant, and walking around the fire. A traditional Indian vegetarian meal will be served soon after the wedding ceremony.
Indian death	During the mourning period—the first 30 to 41 days after the death—observed at the house of the family of the deceased.	Formal wear in sombre, muted colours such as grey, black, and blue.	A wreath, a condolence letter or cash in an envelope.	A short visit with the bereaved family and an opportunity to pay your last respects and say a prayer for the deceased.

Source: Adapted from *Malaysian Customs and Etiquette: A Practical Handbook* by Datin Noor Aini Syed Amir, 2004
Note: Customs may vary depending on individual family beliefs and practices

Percentage of land in Putrajaya dedicated to open, public spaces: 49

NUMBER OF REGISTERED VEHICLES IN MALAYSIA

YEAR	TOTAL
2010	10,746,658
2011	11,415,961
2012	12,112,403
2013	12,670,590
2014	13,471,927
2015	14,430,256
2016	14,936,079
2017	15,565,164
2018	16,230,607
2019	16,892,812
2020	17,486,589
2021	17,728,482

FIRST FAST-FOOD OUTLETS IN MALAYSIA

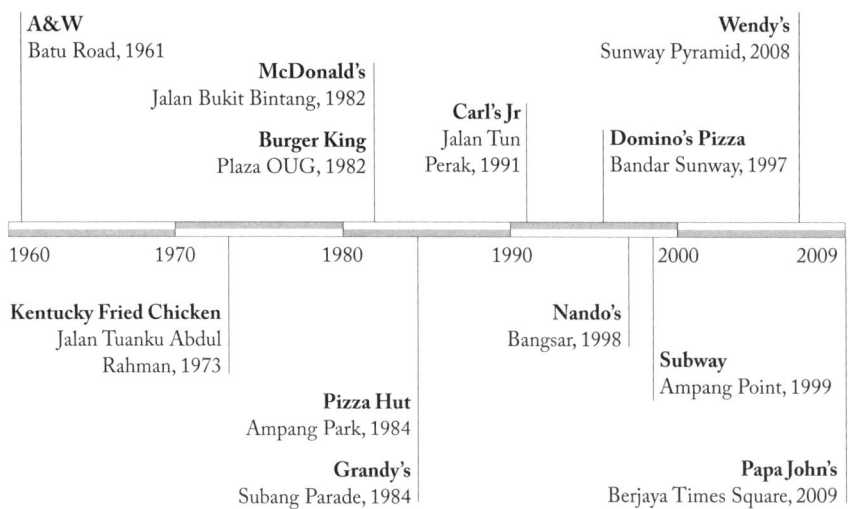

A&W — Batu Road, 1961
McDonald's — Jalan Bukit Bintang, 1982
Burger King — Plaza OUG, 1982
Carl's Jr — Jalan Tun Perak, 1991
Wendy's — Sunway Pyramid, 2008
Domino's Pizza — Bandar Sunway, 1997
Kentucky Fried Chicken — Jalan Tuanku Abdul Rahman, 1973
Pizza Hut — Ampang Park, 1984
Grandy's — Subang Parade, 1984
Nando's — Bangsar, 1998
Subway — Ampang Point, 1999
Papa John's — Berjaya Times Square, 2009

HOW TO GRIP A MALAY KRIS

side view   bottom view

LOST IN TRANSLATION

Subtitles allow viewers to understand a programme filmed in a foreign language. They are also intended to help viewers who are hard of hearing to follow the dialogue. However, occasionally, scripts get misinterpreted and subtitles (as well as translations of movie titles) play an additional role as a source of humour.

Movie/TV Series	English dialogue	Malay subtitle	What it means in English
The Terminator	"Asta Lah Vista Baby."	"*Pemandangan Asta Lah Baby.*"	"The view of Asta Lah Baby."
The Da Vinci Code	"We should toast our victory."	"*Kita patut memberi roti bakar.*"	"We should give away toast."
	"I pray that Jesus will keep me alive."	"*Saya berharap Jesus akan menendang saya...*"	"I hope Jesus will kick me..."
Futurama	Für Elise (by Beethoven)	"*Bulu Elise*"	Elise's fur
	"I won't be able to hear Fry's opera."	"*Saya tidak terdengar opera gorengan.*"	"I can't hear the frying opera."
Rambo: First Blood	"Bring in the chopper!"	"*Bawa kapak!*"	"Get me the axe!"
The Wild Geese	"Duck! Duck!" (to dodge)	"*Itik! Itik!*"	"Duck! Duck!" (the bird)
I Know What You Did Last Summer	"Serial killer"	"*Pembunuh bijirin*"	"Cereal killer"
Cheaper by the Dozen	(Movie title)	Lelong Dua Belas	"Auctioning Twelve"
Finding Nemo	(Movie title)	Lautan Yang Luas	"Wide Ocean"
101 Dalmations	(Movie title)	101 Bintik	"101 Dots"
The Punisher	(Movie title)	Penyeksa	"Torturer"
Sidekicks	(Movie title)	Tendangan Sisi	"To Kick To The Side"

THE KUALA LUMPUR COMPOSITE INDEX

Year	Closing level	Change in index in points	Change in index in %
1976	91.68	6.61	7.77
1977	113.39	21.71	23.68
1978	156.22	42.83	37.77
1979	205.59	49.37	31.60
1980	366.70	161.11	78.36
1981	380.82	14.12	3.85
1982	291.45	-89.37	-23.47
1983	401.60	110.15	37.79
1984	303.56	-98.04	-24.41
1985	233.48	-70.08	-23.09
1986	252.43	18.95	8.12
1987	261.19	8.76	3.47
1988	357.38	96.19	36.83
1989	562.28	204.90	57.33
1990	505.92	-56.36	-10.02
1991	556.22	50.30	9.94
1992	643.96	87.74	15.77
1993	1,275.32	631.36	98.04
1994	971.21	-304.11	-23.85
1995	995.17	23.96	2.47
1996	1,237.96	242.79	24.40
1997	594.44	-643.52	-51.98
1998	586.13	-8.31	-1.40
1999	812.33	226.20	38.59
2000	679.64	-132.69	-16.33
2001	696.09	16.45	2.42
2002	646.32	-49.77	-7.15

Year	Closing level	Change in index in points	Change in index in %
2003	793.94	147.62	22.84
2004	907.43	113.49	14.29
2005	899.79	−7.64	−0.84
2006	1,096.24	196.45	21.83
2007	1,445.03	348.79	31.82
2008	876.75	−568.28	−39.33
2009	1,272.78	396.03	45.17
2010	1,518.91	246.13	19.34
2011	1,530.73	11.82	0.78
2012	1,688.95	158.22	10.34
2013	1,866.96	178.01	10.54
2014	1,761.25	−105.71	−5.66
2015	1,692.51	−68.74	−3.90
2016	1,641.73	−50.78	−3.00
2017	1,796.81	155.08	9.45
2018	1,690.58	−106.23	−5.91
2019	1,588.76	−101.82	−6.02
2020	1,627.21	38.45	2.42

Source: Bursa Malaysia

WILD SEX

- Male and female **orang-utans** stimulate themselves with sex toys made from leaves or twigs. Female orang-utans also attract their partners by hanging from a branch above the males and showing their perineums to the males.

- Female **stalk-eyed flies** are sexually promiscuous and are most attracted to males with stalks so long that their eyes are set farther apart than their bodies are long.

- The mating ritual of **Malayan tapirs** begins with the pair circling one another, nose to rump, and nipping and biting at each other's hind legs and undersides. This action is typically accompanied by snorts and clicks as well as chirps and shrill whistles. Mating takes place on land or in water.

A THORNY ISSUE

Durian cultivars	Physical description	Taste
Chantaburi	Omits odour only after three days	Mild
Chantaburi No. 1	Odourless	Bland
D24	Aromatic, thick and creamy flesh, slightly sticky	Bitter with sweet aftertaste, acrid
D88	Strong-smelling, thick flesh	Sweet, acrid
D101	Sweet, fragrant, smooth reddish flesh, small seeds	Sweet
Jiu Ji	Smooth flesh, small seeds	Sweet
Mao San Wong (also known as Musang King)	Small fruit, thin shell, very fleshy, small seeds, rich yellow flesh, fragrant	Very sweet and creamy
Raja Kunyit	Distinct fragrance, smooth flesh, flat seeds	Sweet, slightly bitter aftertaste
Tawa	Smooth flesh, small seeds	Sweet and acrid
Thraka	Fragrant, small seeds	Sweet and acrid
Udang Merah	Creamy, reddish flesh, small seeds	Sweet
XO	Pungent, served slightly runny	Fermented flavour, mildly bitter

How to pick a quality durian

- Pick up the durian. It should feel light.
- Take a whiff of the fruit. A pungent and almost-sweet smell denotes the seeds inside are ripe and ready to be consumed.
- Avoid durians with crevices on the bottom, which denotes the fruit has over-ripened.

Durian taboos

- Durians, considered by Malaysians to be "heaty", should not be consumed with other "heaty" food or beverages, such as alcohol, coffee, curry or *tom yam*. Doing so can cause serious indigestion.
- Avoid eating the fruit if you have high blood pressure or are pregnant.

Tip

- To rid the pungent odour from your fingers, wash your hands with durian seeds or with water poured into the durian shell.

MISTAKEN IDENTITY?

In February 2009, two identical twin brothers escaped the mandatory death penalty for drug trafficking when the High Court in Kuala Lumpur acquitted and discharged them after ruling that the authorities could not prove which man committed the crime.

The 27-year-old twins, Sathis Raj and Sabarish Raj, had been charged with trafficking 166 kilograms of cannabis and 1.7 kilograms of raw opium in 2003. The police arrested one of the twins when he parked his car outside a house in Kuala Lumpur where authorities found bags of drugs. The second twin arrived later and was also arrested. But, crucially, only the first brother arrested had keys to the house. The police, however, got confused and could not identify which identical twin they arrested first.

"I...can't be sending the wrong person to the gallows," the judge said.

The twins, both clad in white shirts, wept and hugged each other after the judge read the verdict.

Source: The Associated Press, *New Straits Times*

THROWING A TOP

1. The top spinner raises the top, which is wound tightly with string, above his shoulder before taking several quick steps forward.
2. Using great force, the top spinner hurls the top at a 30° angle towards a clay platform.
3. After releasing the top with one hand, the top spinner uses his other hand to pull the string back, thereby giving the top its momentum.

TASIK CHINI LEGENDS

Legend has it that there is a lost Khmer city at the bottom of Tasik Chini, a lake in central Pahang. A couple of expeditions over the decades have found murk and mud. This is the same lake (it's actually 12 linked lakes with a collective name, covering 5,026 hectares, making it the second largest freshwater lake in the country) inhabited by a dragon, the Naga Seri Gumum, if you lend any credence to a legend of the Jakuns, an Orang Asli tribe who roam and live in the area.

INSCRIPTIONS FROM SELECTED TOMBSTONES IN MALACCA

From St Paul's Church
Translated from Dutch

In sacred memory of Madame Joanna Du Moulin, wife of Mr. Bathasar Bort, councillor of the extraordinary territory of India, Governor and Director of the State and fortress of Malacca.
Died on 17th March 1676.

• • •

Here lie the remains of Georgii Cooke, formerly captain of a Dutch vessel. A man of distinguished uprightness, renowned trustworthiness and endowed with various kinds of knowledge.
He died while on his way from China on 16 September in the year of salvation 1712. Aged 36 years.

• • •

Francisca Barbara, most pious wife of Captain Jacobi Barbara, who accompanied her husband on his way from the island of Bombay outside China being great with childbirth. Remained here at Malacca where the period of pregnancy was complete while the hospitable Batavian people vainly laboured for the life and safety of their guest. Before she was relieved of her dread burden, she sank beneath its weight on 10 September 1695.
To dwell with the heavenly host, I left my life, which had been a toil. Death to me was life, in sure and certain hope of resurrection.

From Christ Church
Translated from Armenian

Hail! Thou that read the tablet of my tomb wherein I now do sleep. Give me the news, the freedom of my countrymen, for them I did much weep. If there arose among them one good guardian to govern and to keep. Vainly I expected in the world to see a good shepherd come to look after the scattered sheep.
I, Jacob, grandson of Shameer, an Armenian of a respectable family whose name I keep, was born in a foreign town in Persia, near Inefa, where my parents now forever sleep. Fortune brought me to this distant Malacca, which my remains in bondage doth keep.

• • •

From Christ Church
Translated from Portuguese

This is the grave of Father Ioanno Luius Barboza. Chanter and Vicar of St. Thomas, who died on 24 March 1672.

• • •

This is the grave of Giomar Franco, wife of Di Franco and of their heirs.
Died on 8 March 1562.

From Christ Church
English inscriptions

Sacred to the memory of
James Thomas Fraser
Assistant Surgeon Madras Army
And Residency Surgeon Malacca
Born 2nd September 1827
Died 3rd December 1863
This tablet is erected to his memory by his brother Officers as a mark of their esteem and respect.
"As for man his days are as grass, as a flower of the field, so he flourisheth, for, the wind passeth over it, and it is gone: and the place hereof shall know it no more." Psalm CIII 15, 16.

• • •

Sacred to the memory of the
Rev. William Milne D.D.
For seven years he resided
In this settlement as principal of the Anglo–Chinese College;
Superintending the Education of Chinese and Malay youths
Composing useful and religious tracts
In their respective languages,
And officiating in this church as a
Faithful minister of the Gospel of Christ
But the chief objective of his labours
Was the translation of the
Earliest Protestant version of
The Holy Scriptures in Chinese
He was born in the year 1785,
in Kennethmont, Aberdeenshire, left England as a Missionary, 1812, and died in Malacca June 2nd 1822, at the age of 37.

Sacred to the memory of
Anna Maria,
the beloved wife of Capt.
E.L.M. Evans,
H.M.S. 51st Regiment M.N.I. She was born on the 7th July 1831 and departed this life at Malacca on the 24th January in the year of our Lord 1856 aged 24 years, six months, and seventeen days
Also to the memory of their dear children

Louisa Augusta,
Born 15th April 1851.

Edward Nagle,
Born 12th August 1852.

And Robert Malcolm,
Born 28th October 1855.

They all died at Malacca of diphtheria within 15 days of their poor mother, leaving the bereaved husband and father to bemoan their irreparable loss.

"The Lord gave, and the Lord hath taken away; blessed be the name of the Lord."
Job 1st Chap. 21st Verse.

• • •

To the glory of God and in memory of
Herbert Mitford Derby
21 years Planter in Malaya
Died at Ootacamund Dec. 27, 1915 aged 44 years This tablet was erected by Brother Freemasons as a mark of their great esteem.

Source: *A Short History of Malacca* by Marcus Scott-Ross, 1971

STRAITS SETTLEMENTS LATRINE, 1929

Introduced in the Straits Settlements by Dr Victor G. Heiser, the "bored-hole" latrine was a significant advancement on its predecessor, the "dug pit" latrine.

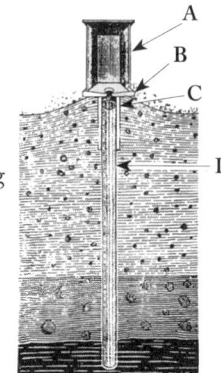

a. Superstructure.
b. Cement slab 30 x 36 inches with a hole in the centre measuring 10–12 x 5.5–6 inches. The edges of the hole were widened to prevent soiling. The surface of the slab slopes toward the hole.
c. Concrete cylinders.
d. Bamboo basket.

Source: *The Malayan Medical Journal and Estate Sanitation*, 1929

COST OF LIVING

Average Monthly Consumption Expenditure, 2019:

Expenditure	Total	Bumiputera	Chinese	Indian
RM	4,534	4,227	5,713	4,760
Food and non-alcoholic beverages	17.3 %	18.9 %	14.3 %	15.8 %
Alcoholic beverages and tobacco	2.3	1.8	3.1	2.8
Clothing and footwear	3.3	3.8	2.7	3.1
Housing, Water, electricity, gas and other fuels	23.6	21.7	25.4	24.7
Furnishings, household items and maintenance	4.4	4.7	4.3	4.1
Health	2.1	2.0	2.5	2.0
Transport	13.5	13.9	13.4	13.1
Communication	5.0	5.1	4.9	5.2
Recreation services and culture	5.1	4.5	6.2	6.2
Education	1.5	1.5	1.5	1.5
Restaurants and hotels	13.9	13.9	13.7	14.0
Miscellaneous goods and services	8.0	8.2	8.0	7.5

Source: Department of Statistics Malaysia

TEN MALAY GHOSTS

Name	Description
orang minyak	The *orang minyak* ("oily man") is a supernatural rapist who, because he is black and slippery, is hard to see and hard to catch. He preys on young women in rural areas.
hantu tetek	The *hantu tetek* ("breast ghost") takes the form of an old woman who kidnaps young children playing outside their houses during the evening prayers and hides them under her cleavage.
orang bunian	Elf-like beings that live in large communities deep in the jungle. Some have been known to assist humans, while others have purportedly abducted people.
kum kum	Believed to be the spirit of an old woman who needs to drink the blood of virgin girls in order to restore her youth and beauty. She is said to knock on doors in her *jibab* (long flowing attire which covers the entire body), saying "*kum kum*" as she is unable to pronounce the Muslim greeting properly.
hantu pocong	Wrapping itself in a white shroud, the *hantu pocong* hops and rolls about wildly. According to Muslim burial practices, when a body is being lowered into the grave, the tie of the shroud must be opened. As legend has it, if the shroud is not opened properly, the corpse will become a *hantu pocong*.
toyol	A *toyol* appears as a naked child with red eyes and sharp teeth. It is kept by a human master in a bottle and trained to steal from others. The master of the *toyol* has to feed it every night by letting it suck blood from his toes.
pelesit	A *pelesit* takes the form of a grasshopper. Mostly reared by women, this ghost is bred to wreak destruction on its master's enemies and obtain money. Every full moon, it feeds on blood from its owner's fingers.
hantu raya	A *hantu raya* is kept by a human master in order to help destroy its master's enemies. It usually assumes the form of its master, but it can also assume the form of other beings. The master must pass it on to another person before he dies or else his corpse will become a zombie.
hantu penanggalan	The *hantu penanggalan* ("ghost of detachment") appears as a woman with the upper half of her body detached from the lower half and her intestines dangling. Her victims are pregnant women and young children.
pontianak	*Pontianak* ("childbearing ghost") is a female vampire who lurks around forests and graveyards. She typically appears as a beautiful and seductive woman, accompanied by a strong scent of frangipani.

Length in metres of the longest satay ever made in Malaysia:

SKY KINGDOM SYMBOLISM

Located in Terengganu, the Sky Kingdom commune was built by the followers of cult leader Ayah Pin. A six-acre, Disneyland-like complex, the commune featured gigantic structures which embodied the cult's beliefs. It was demolished in 2005.

The cream-coloured **teapot** symbolised love pouring from heaven. The ocean-blue **vase** received the water which flowed from the teapot. First-time visitors to the commune would drink the "holy water" from the vase. The **boat** represented Noah's Ark, and the **crescent** stood as a symbol for people who did not subscribe to an organised religion. The **umbrella**, which provided a place for people to take shelter beneath god, was also associated with the nine planets in Hinduism.

AND THE AWARD GOES TO...

Winners of the Boh Cameronian Lifetime Achievement Award:

2002	Krishen Jit (director)
2003	Ramli Ibrahim (dancer, choreographer)
2004	Faridah Merican (actor, director, producer)
2005	Dalang Dollah Baju Merah (mak yong musician, composer)
2006	Dato' Syed Alwi (actor, producer, director, teacher, writer)
2007	Professor Ghulam-Sarwar Yusuf (educator, writer)
2008	Lee Lee Lan (ballerina)

MAS PAYS

In June 2007, national carrier Malaysia Airlines (MAS) was ordered by a Magistrates' Court in Penang to pay RM21,660 to a Brahmin Hindu passenger for wrongly serving him chicken *pakoda* during a flight from Bangalore to Kuala Lumpur in March 2003. A strict vegetarian throughout his entire life, Arvind Sharma aged 44 (a cargo agent for a computer company in India) vomited and experienced depression, shock, stress and humiliation after tasting the chicken.

Source: The Associated Press

A HEATED EXCHANGE

Former Prime Minister Tun Dr Mahathir Mohamad had this testy exchange of correspondence with young Darrell Abercrombie from Camberley Surrey, England. Using his best penmanship, the boy wrote:

> I am 10 years old and when I am older I hope to study animals in the tropical rain forests. But if you let the lumber companys [sic] carry on there will not be any left. And millions of Animals will die. Do you think that is right just so one rich man gets another million pounds or more. I think it is disgraceful.

Dr Mahathir replied on 15 August 1987:

> Dear Darrell,
> It is disgraceful that you should be used by adults for the purpose of trying to shame us because of our extraction of timber from our forests.
> For the information of the adults who use you I would like to say that it is not a question of one rich man making a million pounds....
> The timber industry helps hundreds of thousands of poor people in Malaysia. Are they supposed to remain poor because you want to study tropical animals?....
> When the British ruled Malaysia they burnt millions of acres of Malaysian forests so that they could plant rubber.... Millions of animals died because of the burning. Malaysians got nothing from the felling of the timber. In addition, when the rubber was sold practically all the profit was taken to England. What your father's fathers did was indeed disgraceful.
> If you don't want us to cut down our forests, tell your father to tell the rich countries like Britain to pay more for the timber they buy from us....
> If you are really interested in tropical animals, we have huge National Parks where nobody is allowed to fell trees or kill animals....
> I hope you will tell the adults who made use of you to learn all the facts. They should not be too arrogant and think they know how best to run a country. They should expel all the people living in the British countryside and allow secondary forests to grow and fill these new forests with wolves and bears etc. so you can study them before studying tropical animals.
> I believe strongly that children should learn all about animals and love them. But adults should not teach children to be rude to their elders.

Source: *The Sultan and the Mermaid Queen* by Paul Sochaczewski, 2009

WHEN HAVING BANANA LEAF RICE AT AN INDIAN RESTAURANT...

- Eat with right hand. Utensils are also permitted.
- The narrow side of the leaf will be placed on your left, while the wider side will be on the right. This is so more food can be placed on your right side, since you eat with your right hand.
- When finished, fold the leaf towards you to show you enjoyed your meal. Fold the leaf away from you to show the food was less than satisfactory, or during sombre occasions (funerals).

TRADITIONAL MALAYAN REMEDIES

Medicines for violent headache accompanied by pains in the bones and the loss of vigour.
1. Take (by weight) 5 cents of cumin, 10 cents of garlic, 5 cents of hyoscyamus seeds, 5 cents of Indian hemp, 35 cents of mace, 5 cents of nutmeg, 5 cents of Chinese smilax, 5 cents of ginger and 5 cents of fresh turmeric. Pound them together. Mix with sufficient honey to make into pills. Let the patient take the pills until he has finished them.

Should this fail.
2. Take 2 oz. of goat's brain, saffron and wheat flour; 1 oz. of raw, sticky purple rice, white peppercorns, cinnamon, nutmeg, cloves, curcuma rhizome, coriander seeds, Java long pepper, hyoscyamus seeds, honey, ghee, and opium (a piece the size of a peppercorn); 1/2 oz. of Mossoia bark and 3 oz. of garlic. Grind them together finely. Then cook them together to form a jelly. Let the patient eat this daily, and be relieved.

· · ·

Medicines for numbness of the feet.
1. Take a cupful of the milk of a black goat and a very small cupful of honey. Mix. Drink this on three consecutive mornings.

Should this fail.
2. Take pure gold and pure silver. Rub each three times on stone with honey. Then mix with the aforementioned preparation of milk. Warm slightly and drink.

Source: *The Medical Book of Malayan Medicine*, translated by Ismail Munshi, 1886
Note: The possession and use of opium are strictly prohibited under Malaysian law. (See p. 130)

FOREIGNERS MAKING HEADLINES IN MALAYSIA

To Fail Means Jail! – Dr M Spells Out BN's Options' Sarawak Report (11 November 2022)

'Judge says there is no parliament to attend, rejects Najib's application'
New Straits Times (27 October 2022)

'Only 600,000 of 2.3 million traffic summonses settled in Johor since 2014'
New Straits Times (29 September 2022)

'Malaysia can't afford lockdowns, says health minister' New Straits Times (9 January 2022)

'Mosque built in memory of family of 6 killed in MH17 crash opens'
New Straits Times (14 May 2019)

'Celebrating 100 years of Malaysian palm oil' New Straits Times (19 May 2017)

'Malaysia aims to have varsities in the same league as Oxford, Cambridge within 20 years'
New Straits Times (23 August 2016)

"Frenchman arrested for locking out naked girlfriend" (AFP, 11 February 2009)

"Foreigner killed by exploding homemade firecracker"
(New Straits Times, 4 February 2009)

"Four foreigners nabbed for black money scam" (The Star, 16 January 2009)

"British engineer dies falling off slope" (The Malay Mail, 16 December 2008)

"Bangladeshi: I stole padlock so I'd be deported" (The Star, 6 August 2008)

"Foreigner shot dead when he tried to attack three policemen with a parang"
(The Star, 6 August 2008)

"Australian siblings to help triplets for 18 years" (The Star, 20 July 2008)

"Indonesians held, animal parts seized" (The Star, 5 June 2008)

"Flasher stuns Dutch tourist" (The Star, 10 May 2008)

"Thai PM has one request: A visit to a wet market" (The Star, 21 April 2008)

"Foreigner held for cheating and selling fake honey" (The Star, 19 April 2008)

"No speaky Spanish, so drug case postponed" (The Star, 17 April 2008)

"Religious department defends khalwat raid on American couple" (The Star, 1 November 2006)

"Scientist lost in jungle rescued after phoning UK" (The Independent, 24 March 2005)

"Australian drug traffickers hanged" (New Straits Times, 7 July 1986)

HOW TO IDENTIFY A BORNEO PYGMY ELEPHANT

- Males grow to a height of less than 2.5 metres, compared to other Asian elephants that grow to three metres.
- Longer tail, reaching almost to the ground.
- Straighter tusk.
- Shorter trunk.
- Larger ears.
- Babyish face.
- More rotund.

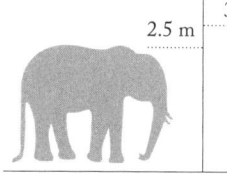
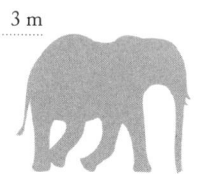

Borneo pygmy elephant   Asian elephant

THE DESIGNER OF THE MALAYSIAN FLAG

The Malaysian flag was designed in 1947 by Mohamed Hamzah, an architect in the Public Works Department. His winning entry was selected through a public poll in the *Malay Mail*. His original design included a five-pointed star, which was later changed to a 14-pointed star to represent all of the Malaysian states and the federal government.

Source: *Going Places*

MALAYSIAN POPULATION STATISTICS

Males	16,805,601 (2021)
Females	15,851,659 (2021)
Persons per square kilometre in Malaysia	96 (2020)
Persons per square kilometre in Kuala Lumpur	8,157 (2020)
Persons per square kilometre in Sarawak	20 (2020)
Persons aged 19 and under	10,435,942 (2021)
Persons aged 20–74	21,476,572 (2021)
Persons aged 75 and over	744,746 (2021)
Live Births	439,744 (2021)
Deaths	224,569 (2021)

Source: *Population and Housing Census*, Department of Statistics Malaysia

THE KILLER

Sepak takraw, a Malaysian national sport, is a fast-paced game that demands physical and mental strength and dexterity. Sepak takraw comprises different moves, one of which is called a "strike". There are many different types of strikes. A good strike or striker is often referred to as the "killer".

Scissor strike–an overhead kick during which the ball gets kicked backward over the player's head.

Foot strike–an effective strike with an element of surprise, executed with the sole of the foot. The player's leg must be outstretched.

Roll strike–an acrobatic kick during which the player rolls in the air and kicks the ball simultaneously. The roll increases the speed of the ball.

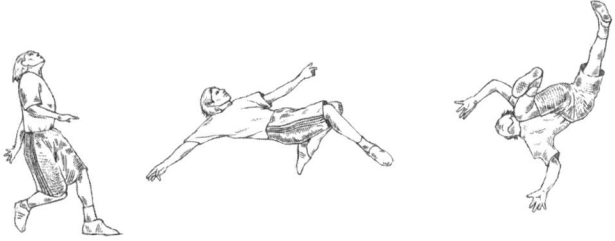

SECRET SOCIETY POETRY

Translated from the original Chinese, the following poems from the Hung secret society in 19th-century Malaya are from a set of 60 poems, many containing covert passwords and messages. Members were required to memorise these poems to instil a sense of solidarity and pride as well as to learn the secret codes of the triad.

> For the oath my finger I prick,
> This is a secret you and I must keep;
> If doing otherwise
> Your suffering is much and deep.

> Red thread goes with red tea,
> Hung man visits only Hung family;
> My brother is now away from home,
> So red tea shall be served by my beloved aunty.

> The sky is covered up by thick, white clouds,
> They must be removed before once again the sky is clear;
> Only the loyal ones can live in brightness,
> Traitors apart the sunlight shall tear.

Source: *The Impact of Chinese Secret Societies in Malaya* by Wilfred Blythe, 1969

TIPS FOR EATING WITH YOUR FINGERS AT A MALAY MEAL

1. Always wash your hands before eating. At formal occasions such as a Malay wedding, a *kendi* (water pot) will be passed around the table for this purpose.
2. Always eat with your right hand (even if you are left-handed). Scoop up the food with the four fingers, and, with your fingers facing your lips, use your thumb to push the food in your mouth. Avoid getting food on the palms of your hands.
3. Each dish which is laid out on the table will have its own serving spoon. Use your left hand to hold the serving spoons.
4. Always wash your hands at the conclusion of the meal.

MAN-EATING MAN

In his memoirs, *The Natives Were Friendly*, Noel Barber, a British novelist and journalist, highlights how friendly and hospitable the "natives" were by remembering a meal of juicy steaks provided by Dayak scouts after they had attacked a Communist camp. His assessment: "a little sweet perhaps". This after the party discovered the steaks had come from the thighs of a Communist sentry killed in the raid, and other more sensitive stomachs had spewed out the meal.

Barber thought nothing of recounting this story to the BBC, which led the British tabloids to have a field day portraying Barber, the brother of the Chancellor of the Exchequer, as a cannibal.

COMPARING COUNTRIES, 2006

Country	Malaysia	Indonesia	Singapore	Japan	UK	USA
Population density per square km	99	143	7.617	330	277	35
Annual population growth rate (%)	1.06	0.81	0.95	-0.37	0.48	0.7
% of population below 15 years	23	26	12	12	18	18
Males per 100 females	103	100	96	94	99	97
Infant mortality rate (per 1000 births)	8.6	23.9	2.5	2.5	4.3	6.5
No. of motor vehicles per 100 persons	54.2	8.2	14.9	62.4	59.4	86.8
Consumer Price Index (% change)	4.48	4.69	7.45	3.0	8.81	7.75
Per capita Gross National Income (USD)	10.93	4.14	64.01	42.62	45.38	70.43

CRIMES AND PUNISHMENTS IN YAP AH LOY'S KUALA LUMPUR, C. 1860

Theft, first offence	paraded through the streets with the stolen goods displayed on the offender's shoulders.
Theft, second offence	the lopping off of one ear.
Murder	execution by running a sword through the throat.

PAVING THE WAY?

When Francis Light landed on the island of Penang in 1786, on the site of the present Esplanade in George Town, the island was virtually uninhabited and covered with dense vegetation. In order to induce his sepoy forces to undertake the arduous work of clearing the site, Light, as legend has it, loaded a cannon with gold coins and fired it into the surrounding jungle. Before long, sufficient land had been cleared for a settlement, and traders and merchants began to arrive.

REACHING FOR THE SKY

Building	Height (m)
Merdeka 118, Kuala Lumpur (2022)	678.9 m
Petronas Twin Towers, Kuala Lumpur (1998)	451.9 m
The Exchange 106, Kuala Lumpur (2019)	445.5 m
Menara Kuala Lumpur, Kuala Lumpur (1996)	421 m
Four Seasons Place, Kuala Lumpur (2018)	342.5 m
Menara Telekom, Kuala Lumpur (2001)	310 m
The Astaka A, Johor Bahru (2018)	279 m
Ilham Tower, Kuala Lumpur (2016)	274 m
Petronas Tower 3, Kuala Lumpur (2012)	267 m
Star Residences ONE, Kuala Lumpur (2019)	265 m
The Astaka B, Johor Bahru (2018)	256 m
Permata Sapura Tower, Kuala Lumpur (2020)	253 m
Trion KL, Kuala Lumpur (2022)	251 m
Star Residences, Kuala Lumpur (2019)	251 m
KOMTAR, George Town (1986, 2016)	249 m
Menara Maybank, Kuala Lumpur (1987)	243.5 m

City	Skyscrapers
Kuala Lumpur	217
Penang	161
Putrajaya	5
Petaling Jaya	3
Subang Jaya	3
Shah Alam	2
Johor Bahru	1
Kota Kinabalu	1
Alor Star	1
Kuching	1

ENGLISH WORDS BORROWED FROM MALAY

- Amok
- Cockatoo [(Burung) Kakak Tua]
- Compound [Kampung]
- Durian
- Gingham
- Gong
- Orang-utan
- Sarong
- Satay

PULSE READING

A traditional Malay healer always begins his examination of a patient by checking the person's pulse. Three fingers (correlating to the three regions of the body) of the healer's right hand rest on the patient's left arm, and, by applying pressure with each finger, the healer can assess the patient's health in the corresponding regions of the body.

Source: *Royal Healer* by Roland Werner, 2002

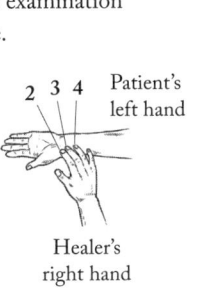

2 3 4 Patient's left hand

Healer's right hand

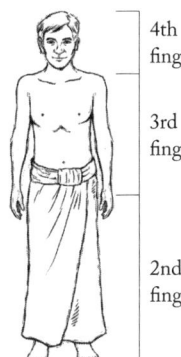

4th finger

3rd finger

2nd finger

THE EFFECTS OF SOME FOODS ACCORDING TO CHINESE MEDICINE

Arrest bleeding	black fungus, chestnut, chicken eggshell, cottonseed, cuttle bone, guava, lotus plumule, spinach, vinegar
Calm down the spirits	liquorice, lily flower
Reduce perspiration	oyster shell, peach
Reduce urination	raspberry
Reduce seminal ejaculation	lotus plumule, oyster shell, walnut, black fungus
Disperse blood coagulation	brown sugar, chive, chive root, crab, hawthorn fruit, saffron, vinegar
Eliminate sputum	Chinese wax gourd, clam, longevity fruit, pear, radish, sea grass, seaweed
Promote milk secretion	common carp, lettuce
Lubricate intestines	apricot seed (bitter and sweet), banana, cow's milk, soybean oil, peach, walnut, watermelon
Promote urination	asparagus, barley, Chinese cabbage, Chinese wax gourd, coffee, corn, corn silk, cucumber, grape, hops, Job's tears, kidney bean
Sharpen vision	abalone, bitter gourd, wild cucumber, freshwater clam, cuttlefish
Tone up the heart	coffee, wheat
Tone up the kidneys	black sesame seed, string bean, sword bean, wheat, kidneys
Tone up the spleen	beef, gold carp, ham, horse bean, hyacinth bean, polished rice, Job's tears
Relieve hot sensations in the body	chicken egg white, crab, mung bean, sea grass

Source: *Chinese System of Food Cures* by Henry C. Lu, 1986

Year in the 1900s when the Malaysian dollar replaced the Malaya and British Borneo dollar:

THE SNAKE TEMPLE

Built in 1850 in Penang, the Snake Temple was originally constructed in honour of the deity of Chor Soo Kong, an ancient Chinese healer and monk. Soon after the temple was constructed, snakes from the surrounding jungle began to congregate there. The snakes were reverently referred to as "blue dragons", and devotees would often plant joss sticks in front of the reptiles.

Today, the temple is still filled with snakes, primarily pit vipers, who, in their natural habitat, are aggressive and venomous. In the Snake Temple, however, they appear docile; it is believed that they are lulled by the smell of the smoke from the burning incense. The temple attracts thousands of visitors annually, but, according to devotees, nobody has ever been bitten.

PROHIBITED COMPANY NAMES IN MALAYSIA

According to the Registration of Businesses Rules 1957, no business—except with the consent of the Minister—shall be registered by a name which:

- contains any word suggesting connection with the Yang di-Pertuan Agong, the Raja Permaisuri Agong or the ruler of a state or a member of the royal family or royal patronage, including such a word as "royal" or any equivalent expression;
- contains any word suggesting connection with the federal or a state government department, statutory body, authority or agency or any municipality or other local authority, including such words as "federal", "state" or "national";
- contains any word suggesting connection with any Asean, Commonwealth or other foreign government or with the United Nations or any other international organization;
- contains the word "chartered" or any words suggesting connection with any Society or body incorporated by Royal Charter;
- contains the words "association", "union", "foundation", "trust", "forces", "co-operative", "international" or any equivalent expression;
- contains any word that is blasphemous or likely to be offensive to members of the public;
- contains any word that is misleading as to the nature, scope or importance of the business carried on or to be carried on under such name;
- contains any word that is offensive to any race or religion.

Source: Suruhanjaya Syarikat Malaysia

TYPES OF MALAYSIAN TIMBER

Types of timber	Average density (kg/m^3)	Value (per m^3)	Uses
Heavy hardwood			
Chengal	915–980	RM5,000	Heavy construction, railway sleepers, heavy-duty furniture, bridges, telegraphic and power transmission posts and cross arms, piling, heavy traffic flooring, heavy-duty columns
Balau	850–1,155	RM3,030	Heavy construction, marine construction, ship and boat building, piling, beams, bridges, wharves, heavy-traffic flooring, decking, heavy-duty furniture
Merbau	515–1,040	RM3,250	Heavy-traffic flooring, superior joinery, musical instruments, carvings, reproduction antique furniture, heavy-duty furniture, heavy permanent-type pallets
Medium hardwood			
Keruing	595–945	RM1,970	Heavy construction, posts, beams, joists, rafters, ship and boat building, vehicle bodies, container flooring, harbour works, bridges, telegraph poles
Kapur	580–820	RM1,930	Medium construction, door and window frames and sills, fender supports, flooring, staircase, vehicle bodies, ship and boat building, laboratory benches
Light hardwood			
Dark Red Meranti	415–885	RM2,185	Joinery, furniture, high-class interior finishing, fancy doors, door and window frames and sills, vehicle bodies, ship and boat building, cooling towers and other constructional works
Nyatoh	400–1,075	RM1,420	Furniture, solid doors, high-class decorative works and interior finishing, light duty columns, vehicle bodies, ship and boat building, railway sleepers, tool handles
Jelutong	420–500	RM1,075	Pencil manufacturing, boxes and crates, disposable chopsticks, toothpicks, picture frames, drawing boards, blackboards, battery separators, toys, wooden shoe heels
Rubberwood	560–640	RM225	Charcoal manufacturing, core material for block board, pulp and paper manufacturing, production of medium density fibrewood. Possible end use is the manufacture of rayon

Note: On average, 60% of the above types of timber are exported, while the rest are used in the domestic market. Timber logs measure 18 inches and above in diameter and 12 feet and above in length.
Source: Malaysian Timber Industry Board

POOR THAMBY WORKS ON THE RAILWAY

In 1885, me khaki breeches I put on.
Me khaki breeches I put on,
to work on the railway, the railway.
I'm weary of the railway.

Poor Thamby works on the Railway.
In 1886, for Port Weld I moved to Klang,
and found myself a job to do
a working on the Railway.

Chorus:
I was wearing khaki breeches,
digging ditches,
pulling switches,
dodging hitches,
I was working on the railway.

In 1903, I broke me a shovel across my knees
And went to work for the company
On the Johore Government Railway.

Chorus

In 1924, I landed on the Kelantan shore
Me belly was empty

And me hands were raw with
Working on the Railway, the Railway
I'm weary of the Railway.

Poor Thamby works on the Railway.
In 1925, when Ramasamy Muthusamy
He was alive, when Ramasamy Muthusamy
He was alive, working on the Railway.

Chorus

In 1936, I changed me trade from
carrying cups.
Changed me trade from carrying cups
To working on the Railway.

Chorus

In 1942, poor Thamby was thinking
of going to heaven, Poor Thamby was
thinking of going to heaven,
And working on the Railway,
The Siam railway.
I'm weary of the railway,
Poor Thamby works on the Railway.

Source: *The Underside of Malaysian History* by Peter Rimmer and Lisa Allen, 1990

THE CONCEPT OF THE SOUL

The Orang Asli Jah-Het tribe believe that the soul of every human being is a bird called a *biau*, which has a long beak and feeds on fruits and insects. The *biau* has two cries: one *kah-kah-kah* and the other *tutuh buah*. When a woman is pregnant and hears one of these birds in the jungle, she knows that the soul of her child has arrived. When a human dies, his soul leaves him in the form of a *biau*. If anyone catches a *biau*, a great thunderstorm occurs.

Source: *Jah-het of Malaysia, Art and Culture* by Roland Werner, 1975

SOME TRADITIONAL MALAY REMEDIES FOR FEVER

- A banana
- Fine rice dust
- Fresh turmeric

The ingredients are to be ground, mixed, and taken internally on four consecutive mornings.

- The tail of a white pigeon
- Python's bile

The ingredients are rubbed on a stone slab with a little water and taken internally.

- Rancid brinjal
- Sour vinegar

The ingredients are to be mixed and consumed.

- Sulphur
- Red sandalwood
- The horn of a sambhur deer
- Flour
- Elephant's tusk

The ingredients are to be rubbed on a stone slab with a little water and taken internally.

Source: *Royal Healer* by Roland Werner, 2002

A MALACCA TOWNHOUSE

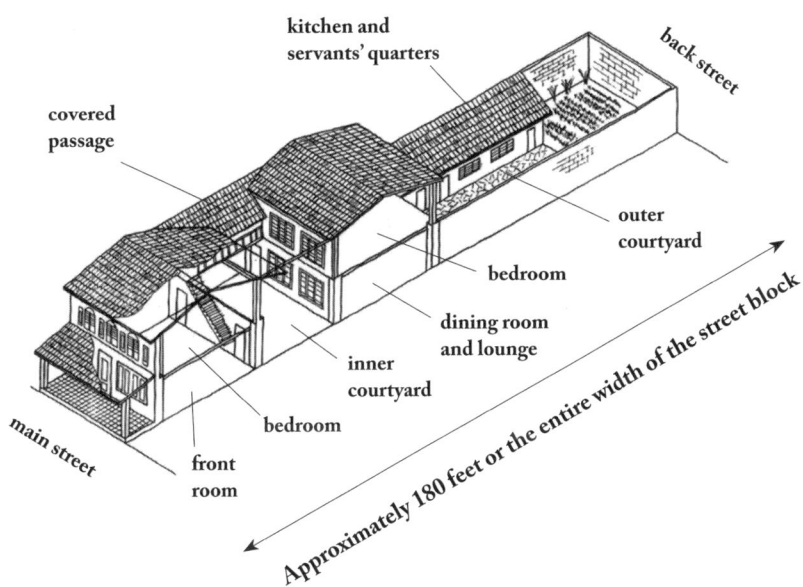

BUNGLED BURGLARIES

In 2008, two burglars admitted to mistakenly entering a bank in Kota Bharu, Kelantan while attempting to enter a building that was used to breed swiftlets, which were kept for their profitable nests. The Kota Bharu police district chief told reporters that the men were caught with the help of a bank security guard at about 11.30 p.m. and had with them various pieces of equipment for breaking and entering a building. "They admitted to wanting to steal the birds' nests but mistakenly entered the bank and were caught by a patrol unit," he said. The two burglars were investigated under Section 448 of the Penal Code for breaking into a bank.

• • •

A burglar claimed he was held captive by a "supernatural figure" for three days in December 2008, when he broke into a house-turned-grocery-store in the town of Kemaman, Terengganu. Having realised the owners of the house were away, the intruder forced his way into the house and claimed he was blinded once inside. "Each time I wanted to flee, I felt a "supernatural figure" shoving me to the ground," he told the police. The owners of the house returned three days later to find the intruder fatigued and dehydrated, his hands clasped in an apologetic gesture for his misdeed. Instead of calling the police, the owners called for an ambulance. The couple lodged a police report on the same day. It was reported a few days later that the shop owner denied any claims of sorcery, but claimed that it must have been divine intervention.

• • •

Police in Kuala Lumpur detained an eight-member gang of small-sized robbers dubbed the "midget gang", who allegedly confessed to committing 14 break-ins over the past three months. All the gang members—aged between 14 and 23 years—were diminutive. Some of them who were less than 5 feet tall would be picked to squeeze through small openings into the houses they robbed. The arrests occurred after residents in a housing area noticed the group loitering suspiciously in a field near their homes and alerted the police.

• • •

A 53-year-old Chinese man in Penang was arrested after shoplifting two bottles of gin worth RM91.98 from a supermarket in 2007. When he was charged in magistrates' court, though, the thief claimed that he believed the supermarket belonged to him. "I didn't steal," the man argued before the judge, "I heard voices telling me to go and take the bottles. The supermarket is mine, how can that be considered stealing?" The man wanted to plead guilty to the shoplifting charges, but the court ruled that since a psychiatric report had established that he was of unsound mind, he would be sent back to live in a psychiatric institution.

Source: Bernama (Malaysian national news agency), *The Star*, The Associated Press

HOW A TIN DREDGE WORKED

Tin was one of the pillars of the pre-Independence economy. The most effective and capital intensive method of mining alluvial tin, tin dredges were used throughout the 20th century in low-lying areas with tin deposits. Tin dredges, however, are no longer used in Malaysia.

1. The dredge floated on a natural or artificial lake.
2. A chain of massive buckets dug as deep as 30 to 40 metres, scooping out the earth-bearing ore from the lake.
3. The earth-bearing ore was carried to a high point in the body of the dredge.
4. The excavated material was broken up by jets of water as it fell onto revolving or oscillating screens. Large stones and rubble were retained by these screens while material bearing tin ore passed through the holes in the screen and was collected in a tank below the screens. The tin ore was then separated, using water pumps, from foreign matter and cleaned.
5. The purified tin ore was collected in drums to be transported from the dredge to the treatment plant.
6. Mud, sand, clay and gravel were discharged with the main flow of water and were dumped in the tailings area at the rear of the dredge.

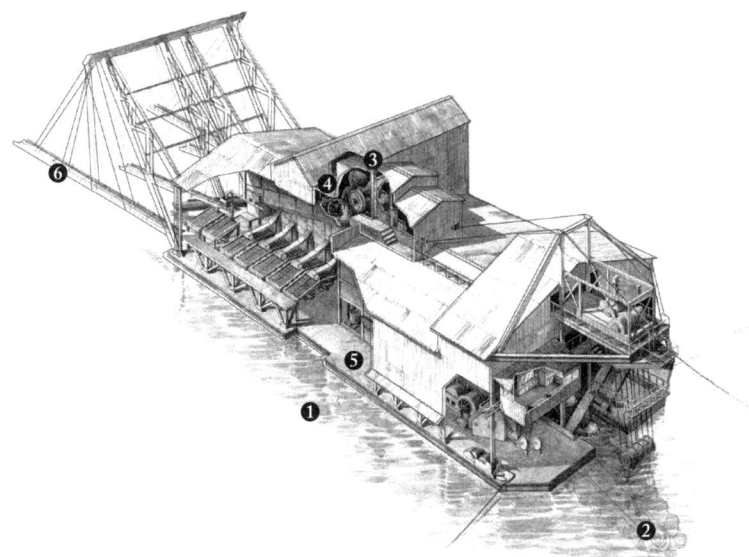

MALAYSIANS WHO HAVE APPEARED ON STAMPS

Name	Description	Stamp date
Rulers		
Sultan Abu Bakar	Ruler	2020
Sultan Abdul Halim Mu'adzam Shah	Ruler	2016
Sultan Abdullah Ri'ayatuddin	Ruler	2019
Sultan Azlan Muhibbuddin Shah	Ruler	1990, 2002, 2009
Sultan Ahmad Shah Sultana Kalsom	Ruler	1980, 2010, 2014
Sultan Haji Ahmad Shah	Ruler	1980
Sultan Hisamuddin Alam Shah	Ruler	1960, 1967, 2002
Sultan Ibrahim Iskandar	Ruler	2015
Sultan Iskandar Ismail	Ruler	1984, 2002
Sultan Ismail Nasiruddin Shah	Ruler	1966, 1967, 2002
Sultan Muhammad V	Ruler	2017
Sultan Nazrin Muizzuddin	Ruler	2015
Sultan Sallehuddin	Ruler	2018
Sultan Salahuddin Abdul Aziz	Ruler	1999, 2002
Sultan Yahya Petra	Ruler	1976
Tuanku Abdul Halim	Ruler	1971, 2002, 2008, 2012
Tuanku Abdul Rahman	Ruler	1957, 1967, 2002
Tuanku Jaafar	Ruler	1994, 2002, 2007
Tuanku Mizan Zainal Abidin	Ruler	2007
Tuanku Syed Putra	Ruler	1960, 1967, 2002
Tuanku Syed Sirajuddin	Ruler	2002
Politicians		
Tunku Abdul Rahman Putra	Prime Minister	1957, 1969, 1991, 2003, 2007, 2013, 2020
Tun Abdul Razak	Prime Minister	1977, 1991, 2007
Tun Abdullah Ahmad Badawi	Prime Minister	2007
Tun Hussein Onn	Prime Minister	1991, 2007
Tun Dr Mahathir Mohamad	Prime Minister	1998, 2007
Dato' Onn Jaafar	Politician	2007
Tun V. T. Sambanthan	Politician	2007
Tun Tan Cheng Lock	Politician	2007

Name	Description	Stamp date
Sportspersons		
Cheah Soon Kit	Badminton player	1992, 1998
Choong Tan Fook	Badminton player	1998
Foo Kok Keong	Badminton player	1992
Jalani Sidek	Badminton player	1992
Kwan Yoke Meng	Badminton player	1992
Lee Wan Wah	Badminton player	1992, 1998
Ong Ewe Hock	Badminton player	1998
Rahman Sidek	Badminton player	1992
Rashid Sidek	Badminton player	1992
Razif Sidek	Badminton player	1992
Soo Beng Kiang	Badminton player	1992
Wong Choon Hann	Badminton player	1998
Wong Ewee Mun	Badminton player	1992
Yap Kim Hock	Badminton player	1998
Yong Hock Kin	Badminton player	1998
Sapok Biki	Boxer	1998
Dato' Khalid Mohd Yunus	Commonwealth Games Chef-de-mission	1998
Carolyn Au Yong	Gymnast	1998
El Regina Tajuddin	Gymnast	1998
Sarina Sundarajah	Gymnast	1998
Thye Chee Kiat	Gymnast	1998
M. Magendran	Mountain climber	2000
N. Mohanadas	Mountain climber	2000
Abdul Latif Romly	Paralympian (shot put)	2016
Mohamed Ridzuan Mohamed Puzi	Paralympian (runner)	2016
Muhammad Ziyad Zolkelfi	Paralympian (long jump)	2016
Govindasamy Saravanan	Race walker	1998
Dato' Azhar Mansor	Sailor	2000
Nurul Huda Bahrain	Sport shooter	1998
Kenny Ang Ah Tee	Tenpin bowler	1998
Ben Heng Boon Hian	Tenpin bowler	1998
Gerald Read	Trekker	2000

Highest FIFA ranking by the national football team, in 1993:

Name	Description	Stamp date
Justin Read	Trekker	2000
Muhamad Hidayat Hamidon	Weightlifter	1998
Others		
P. Ramlee	Artist and entertainer	1999
Datuk Sheikh Muszaphar Shukor	Astronaut	2008
Hang Tuah	Folk hero	2014
Kamaludin bin Muhammad	National Laureate	2016
Muhammad bin Abdul Biang	National Laureate	2016
Usman bin Awang	National Laureate	2016
Tun Siti Hasmah Mohamad Ali	Prime Minister's wife	1998
Zainal Abidin Ahmad (Za'ba)	Scholar	2002
Sultana Kalsom	Wife of Ruler	2010

SELECTED WILDLIFE-RELATED CRIMES AND PUNISHMENTS

Killing a tiger
— fine of up to RM15,000 and/or up to five years imprisonment

Killing a tapir
— fine of up to RM5,000 and/or five years imprisonment.

Failure to comply with an anti-rabies vaccination order on dogs
— fine of RM250

Cruelty to animals
— fine of RM200,000 and/or up to six months imprisonment (major increase in 2015)

Counterfeiting, copying, altering, defacing or erasing any brand or mark applied by a veterinary authority
— fine of RM200

Failing to comply with a veterinary authority's order to disinfect a stable, shed, cage, pen or other place in which an infected animal or bird has been found or kept
— fine of RM100

Possession of unsterilised bull over 15 months of age in Kedah or Kelantan
— fine of RM100

SALARIES 2018 OF MINISTERS AND SENIOR CIVIL SERVANTS

Ministers/Senior civil servants	Monthly salary (RM)
Cabinet/Administration	
• Prime Minister	22,826.65
• Deputy Prime Minister	18,168.15
• Minister	14,907.20
• Deputy Minister	10,847.65
• Parliamentary Secretary	7,187.40
• Member of the Parliamentary	16,000.00
Dewan Rakyat (House of Representatives)	
• Speaker	14,907.20
• Deputy Speaker	10,847.65
• Opposition Leader	3,846.59
• Leader–House of Representatives	3,846.59
• Deputy Leader–House of Representatives	1,983.19
• Member of the House of Representatives	16,000.00
Dewan Negara (Senate)	
• President	14,902.20
• Deputy President	10,847.65
• Member of the Senate	11,000.00

Source: Members of Parliament (Remuneration) Act 1980 (Amended 2007)

MAN HIT WITH RM806 TRILLION PHONE BILL

In April 2006, Yahaya Wahab from Kedah nearly fainted when he received a phone bill for RM806,400,000,000,000.01 (US$218 trillion) and was ordered to pay up within 10 days or face prosecution. Wahab said he disconnected his late father's phone line in January 2006 after he died and settled the RM84 phone bill, but Telekom Malaysia later sent him the hefty invoice. It wasn't clear whether the bill was a mistake, or if Yahaya's father's phone line was used illegally after his death.

Source: The Associated Press

SEXUAL HEALING

 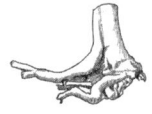

For her: *Kacip fatimah* (*Labisia pumila*) is traditionally used by Malay women to enhance sexual function as it increases testosterone levels, as well as to maintain a healthy reproductive system and to ease menopausal symptoms.

For him: *Tongkat ali* (*Eurycoma longifolia* Jack) is a herb famed for its aphrodisiac properties. Additionally, it is reported to reduce stress and enhance one's sense of well-being.

USES OF CANNONS IN THE MALAY PENINSULA AND BORNEO

1. **Decoration**—cannons were used to decorate boats.
2. **Fighting and defence**—boats and fortresses were equipped with cannons to defend themselves against attack.
3. **Communication**—cannons were fired as a warning or signal as well as to transmit messages (announcement of a birth, death, or festival) and to drive away evil spirits.
4. **Marking royal occasions**—cannons were used to mark royal ceremonies such as births, deaths, coronations, award ceremonies, and weddings.
5. **Currency**—miniature cannons were used as currency in Borneo in the trading of goods and the settlement of fines.

NAMING A CHILD

In the Iban community of Sarawak, before a newborn baby is named, he or she is affectionately called *ulat* (worm), irrespective of his or her gender. The infant's parents and relatives must name the child after his or her lineal great grandparents or the great grandparents' brothers, sisters or cousins, provided the original name bearer is already dead. The name of a living person cannot be given to the baby for fear that doing so might shorten the life of that person. When a few names have been selected, rice balls are made, each representing a name. The first rice ball pecked at by a *manok tawai* (fighting cock) determines the child's name.

TRADITIONAL WEIGHTS AND MEASURES

Before the metric system was officially adopted in Malaysia in 1982, traditional weights and measures were commonly used in the country.

Local units	Metric equivalent	Imperial equivalent
Weights		
1 chupak	1.14 litres	1 quart
1 gantang	4.55 litres	1 gallon
1 nalih	72.74 litres	16 gallons
1 kuncha	727.38 litres	160 gallons
1 hun	0.377 grams	0.013 ounces
1 chi	3.77 grams	0.13 ounces
1 tahil	37.79 grams	1.33 ounces
1 kati	0.60 kilograms	1.33 pounds
1 gantang of padi	2.27 kilograms	5 pounds approximately
1 gantang of rice (milled)	3.63 kilograms	8 pounds approximately
1 pikul	60.47 kilograms	133.33 pounds
1 bahara	181.44 kilograms	400 pounds
1 koyan	2.419 tonnes	5,333.33 pounds
Length		
1 kaki	0.3048 metres	12 inches
1 hasta	0.4572 metres	1.5 feet
1 jengkal	0.2286 metres	0.75 feet (½ hasta)
1 ela	0.9144 metres	3 feet
1 depa	1.829 metres	6 feet
1 depa	1.609 kilometres	0.99 miles
Area		
(only used in Kedah and Perlis)		
1 jemba	5.946 square metres	64 square feet
1 relong	0.287 square kilometres	71 acres
(only used in Kelantan)		
1 square depa	4.047 square metres	43.56 square feet
1,000 square depa	4,046.86 square metres	1 acre

Number of medals won by Malaya/Malaysia at the 1961 Rangoon Asian Games (and also the 1969 Rangoon Asian Games):

SCHOOL MOTTOS

School	Location	Colours	Motto
Penang Free School 1816	George Town	White and azure (blue)	*Fortis Atque Fidelis* Strong and Faithful (Latin)
Malacca High School 1826	Melaka	Mauve and green	*Meliora Hic Sequamur* Here we strive for better things (Latin)
St Thomas School 1848	Kuching	Black and red	Aim Higher
St Xavier's Institution 1852	George Town	Green and gold	*Labor Omnia Vincit* Labour Conquers All (Latin)
St Francis' Institution 1880	Melaka	Green and white	*Age quod agis* Whatever you do, do it well (Latin)
King Edward VII School 1883	Taiping	Red and Black	*Magni Nominis Umbra* Under the shadow of a Great Name (Latin)
Bukit Bintang Girls' School 1893	Kuala Lumpur	Green and white	*Nisi Dominus Frustra* Without God, All is in vain (Latin)
Victoria Institution 1893	Kuala Lumpur	Oxford blue and Cambridge blue	Be Yet Wiser
St Paul's Institution 1899	Seremban	Green and white	*Virtute et labore* Virtue and labour (Latin)
St John's Institution 1904	Kuala Lumpur	Gold and green	Fide et labore Faith and Labour (Latin)
The Malay College Kuala Kangsar 1905	Perak	White, red, black, yellow	*Fiat Sapientia Virtus* Manliness Through Wisdom (Latin)
Confucian Private Secondary School 1906	Kuala Lumpur	Red, black, sky blue and white	-
Thamboosamy Pillay Primary School 1906	Kuala Lumpur	-	-
St Michael's Institution 1912	Ipoh	Green and white	*Quis ut Deus?* Who [is] like God? (Latin)
Chung Hwa High School 1912	Muar	-	-
Sultan Abu Bakar Complex Secondary School 1914	Johor Bahru	Yellow and green	*Berilmu Berwawasan* With Knowledge And Vision (Malay)
St George's Institution 1915	Taiping	Green and white	*Honor virtutis praemium* Honor is the reward for virtue (Latin)
Maxwell School c.1917	Kuala Lumpur	Royal green, yellow and blue	Disco Ut Serviam I Learn That I May Serve (Latin)

King George V School 1923	Seremban	Blue, white and red	*Veni, Vidi, Vici* I Came, I Saw, I Conquered (Latin)
Bukit Mertajam High School 1927	Penang	Red, white and black	*Aut Coepisse Noli Aut Confice* Accomplish Or Do Not Begin (Latin)
Sam Tet Secondary School 1934	Ipoh	Blue, yellow and white	-
The Alice Smith School 1946	Kuala Lumpur	-	*Sic Itur Ad Astra* In This Way You Shall Go To The Stars (Latin)
Garden International School 1951	Kuantan	-	*Plus Est En Vous* There Is More Within You (French)
Cochrane Secondary School 1957	Kuala Lumpur	-	*Satu Untuk Semua, Semua Untuk Satu* One For All, All For One (Malay)

A LETTER TO THE KING

Excerpts of a letter from Afonso De Albuquerque, the Portuguese conqueror of Malacca, to the King of Portugal.

20 August 1512

Malacca was taken by force for not accepting conditions for peace.

Your Highness had said that at all costs we should make an accord with Malacca. They refused to accept your trade or your request for peace, and did not consider us as men who were fit to place our feet on their land. They thought that their fleet which they had built would destroy us. They fortified themselves on land and trusted that the monsoon which was coming soon would force us to leave their port. They were at times aggressive towards us and considered us merely as eight hundred men, and I believe, despised us as nothing more than white men.

It pleased Our Lord and Our Blessed Lady to give us complete victory over them. Even after several messages were exchanged, and after protestations were made by me and after defeating him once, the Sultan refused to accept any accord which would have given him back the town undamaged.

It appears that the affair of Malacca seems to have been ordained by God, for they failed to keep it in spite of the enormous wealth they possessed, either by a trade agreement or a treaty with Your Highness, or by force of arms and artillery, which they had in great abundance.

The number of Russian sailors killed in the Battle of Penang in 1914:

HAND DANCE

The following hand gestures are commonly used in traditional Malay dances.

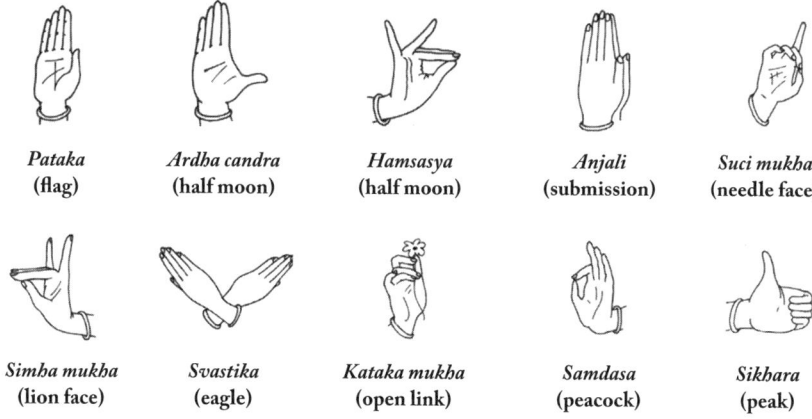

| Pataka (flag) | Ardha candra (half moon) | Hamsasya (half moon) | Anjali (submission) | Suci mukha (needle face) |

| Simha mukha (lion face) | Svastika (eagle) | Kataka mukha (open link) | Samdasa (peacock) | Sikhara (peak) |

HOW TO EXECUTE A SIDEK SERVE

1. Hold the shuttlecock upside down with the feathers facing the racket.
2. Strike the shuttlecock feathers with the racket
   or
   Strike the shuttlecock feathers and then the base (cork) of the shuttlecock.
3. Slice the shuttlecock into the opponent's court, resulting in a serve with a wild and unpredictable flight pattern.

Note: The dreaded Sidek serve was invented by the Sidek brothers—Malaysian badminton greats—in the early 1980s. Because of the serve's effectiveness, it was indirectly banned by the International Badminton Federation which introduced rule 9.1.4 ("During the service the racket shall initially hit the base (cork) of the shuttlecock").

THE ONLY JEWISH CEMETERY

The country's only Jewish cemetery is located on Jalan Zainal Abidin, formerly Yahudi Road, in Penang. The 3,538 m² plot has 106 graves, the oldest dating from 1835 and the most recent dating from 2011.

Source: *New Straits Times*

THE RAMLY DOUBLE SPECIAL CHEESE BURGER

The Ramly Burger company was incorporated in 1984 under the leadership of Tuan Haji Ramly Mokni and Puan Hajjah Shala Siah, who strongly advocated pureness in the production of "halal", clean and quality products. The Ramly Double Special Cheese Burger—comprising two burger patties, an egg and a slice of cheese—has become one of the most popular fast-food snacks in Malaysia. Ramly Burger stalls usually open at night until the wee hours—and during the day as well.

Buns—High-protein wheat flour, purified water, sugar, vegetable fat (palm oil), baker's yeast, salt, contains permitted dough conditioners (emulsifiers and enzymes), skimmed milk powder, permitted food preservative (E282).

Mayonnaise—soya bean oil, eggs, sugar, vinegar, salt, citric acid, preservative, lemon juice, flavouring (contains peanuts), xanthan gum, calcium disodium ETA.

Chilli sauce—Sugar, chillies, salt, tomato paste, garlic, spice, contains permitted flood conditioners.

Worcestershire sauce—vinegar, molasses, sugar, salt, anchovies, tamarind extract, onions, garlic, spice, flavouring.

Margarine—palm oil, palm kernel oil, palm fractions, sunflower oil, water, salt and vitamins, contains permitted food conditioners, flavouring substances, antioxidants and colouring substances.

Cheese slice—Cheese, butter milk powder, whey powder, sodium citrate (331), sodium phosphates (452, 339), citric acid (330), preservative (202), natural annatto (160b), water added.

Ground white pepper.

Beef or chicken burger patties—Beef or chicken, soy protein, spices and salt, flavouring and food conditioners.

Chicken egg.

Vegetables—shredded or sliced cabbage or lettuce and sliced onions.

Did you know?
Fresh Ramly Burger patties are banned in Singapore, but frozen patties are approved for sale in the island-state.

Year in the 1900s when Malaysia's first Islamic bank, Bank Islam Malaysia Berhad (BIMB), was established: 85

SOME OF THE PRIME MINISTERS' FAVOURITE FOODS

1. **Tunku Abdul Rahman Putra**
   Roast beef and Yorkshire pudding, Chinese steamboat, *ayam golek* (spicy roasted chicken), *daging bakar air asam* (roasted meat)

2. **Tun Abdul Razak Hussein**
   Curried patin fish, roast beef with Sarawak black pepper sauce, tomato rice with chicken kurma, *ikan asam pedas* (sour and spicy fish), chicken kuzi, *agar-agar* (jelly), *sambal* green pepper and *otak-otak* (grilled fish paste), Yorkshire pudding, butter pudding

3. **Tun Hussein Onn**
   French bread with bean sauce, chicken pie, *laksa* Johor and *pilah* chicken rice

4. **Tun Dr Mahathir Mohamad**
   Curried crab, beef with black pepper sauce and beef rice

5. **Tun Abdullah Ahmad Badawi**
   *Udang goreng asa*m (fried asam prawns), *nasi tomato* (tomato rice), *laksa, kuih ketayap inti kelapa* (pancake with coconut filling), *pulut seri muka* (a local cake), *kuih talam* (a local cake), *dadih* (sweet yogurt) and *kuih gedong chak* (grilled cake made of glutinous rice)

6. **Dato' Sri Najib Tun Razak**
   Roti canai, sambal tumis telur (egg chilli paste), *ikan patin masak tempoyak cili padi* (patin fish cooked with fermented durian and fire chillies)

7. **Najib**
   Also the Super Ring cheesy snack.

8. **Tan Sri Dato Haji Muhyiddin Yassin**
   Unknown

9. **Dato Sri Ismail Sabri Yaacob**
   Unknown

10. **Anwar Ibrahim**
    Peshwari lamb kebab.

"RINGGIT"

The word "ringgit", which means "jagged" in Malay, originally referred to the serrated edges of the Spanish silver dollars that were widely circulated in Southeast Asia.

Source: *New Straits Times*

THE WORLD'S LARGEST LEAF

The world's largest undivided leaf comes from the *Alocasia macrorrhiza* plant, indigenous to Sabah. A specimen found in 1966 was 3.02 metres long and 1.92 metres wide.

Source: *New Straits Times*

SPIDERMAN VERSUS THE PETRONAS TWIN TOWERS

Frenchman Alain Robert—known as "Spiderman" because he has climbed more than 70 skyscrapers worldwide without using ropes or safety equipment—successfully scaled the 452-metre Petronas Twin Towers on the morning of 1 September 2009. It took the 47-year-old just over two hours to complete his ascent, and when he reached the pinnacle he unfurled a Malaysian flag and waved his arms in celebration. When he re-entered the building on the 88th floor, however, he was arrested by local police and charged with criminal trespass. "Spiderman" had made two previous attempts to scale the Petronas Twin Towers, but was intercepted by local authorities.

Year of attempt	Floor reached	Outcome
1997	60 (Tower 1)	Arrested by police. Freed without charge.
2007	60 (Tower 2)	Arrested by police. Freed without charge.
2009	88 (Tower 2)	Arrested by police and charged with criminal trespass after reaching the top of the skyscraper. He pleaded guilty and was fined RM2,000. He also promised never to climb another building in Kuala Lumpur again.

Source: *The Star*

SOME MALAYSIAN FIRSTS

1806	The first **English-language newspaper**, The Prince of Wales Island Gazette, is published.
1807	The first **police squad** is set up in Penang.
1816	The first **English school**, the Penang Free School, is founded by Reverend Sparke Hutchings.
1870	The first **swimming pool**, the Coronation Swimming Pool, is opened in Perak.
1876	The first **telegraph line** is completed in Perak, stretching 44 km from the Resident's office in Kuala Kangsar to the Assistant Resident's office in Taiping.
1879	The first **prison**, the Taiping Gaol, is opened in Perak.
1880	The first **general hospital**, the Taiping General Hospital, is established.
1882	The first **library**, the Reading and Recreation Room for Officers, is opened in Taiping.
1883	The first **fire and rescue squad** is formed in Selangor.
1883	The first **museum**, the Perak Museum, is opened in Taiping.
1884	The first **post office** is established in Taiping.
1885	The first **railway line**, running between Taiping and Port Weld, is opened in Perak.
1891	The first **telephone exchange** is installed in Kuala Lumpur.
1898	The first **dam**, the Air Keroh Dam in Malacca, is built.
1900	The first **power station**, a hydro-powered station built to operate a gold mine, is opened in Pahang.
1910	The first **oil well**, subsequently named 'The Grand Old Lady', is sunk by Shell in Miri, Sarawak.
1924	The first **commercial aircraft**, a Fokker F27 on its way from Amsterdam to Jakarta, lands on a bumpy strip in Alor Star, Kedah.
1931	The first **radio broadcasts** are introduced for three days each week from 6.30 p.m. to 8.30 p.m.
1936	The first **cinema**, the Pavilion Theatre, is opened in Kuala Lumpur with 1,200 seats.
1937	The first **telephone call** from Malaya to London.
1963	The first **television transmission** is made by Radio Television Malaysia (RTM).
1967	The first **night market**, accomodating 135 stalls, opens on Jalan Ampang in Kuala Lumpur.
1974	The first **tolled expressway**, the Tanjung Malim–Slim River Toll Road, is completed.

1985	The first **national car**, the Proton Saga, rolls out from a manufacturing plant in Shah Alam.
1996	The first **national motorcycle**, the Modenas Kriss, is produced.
1999	The first **underground railway line**, the Putra LRT, commences operations. The underground section stretches 4.4 km.
2009	The first **submarine**, the KD Tunku Abdul Rahman, sails from France to Port Klang.

FENG SHUI IN ACTION

The 38-room Cheong Fatt Tze mansion in Penang was built between 1897 and 1904 according to Feng Shui principles. A gathering of Feng Shui practitioners was held in the house in the mid-1990s and they were all unable to find any fault with the design.

- The main door is aligned to face south–southeast.
- Hills at the back and sea at the front of the house.
- The back of the house is raised higher than the front, to create a feeling of ascendancy.
- Rainwater falling on the roofs around the central courtyard is collected via two drainpipes encased in walls and allowed to accumulate temporarily in the sunken, granite slab-lined courtyard. This drainage system is important because it facilitates the accumulation of *qi*, the slow accumulation of water is likened to the slow amassing of wealth, and the direction of the water flow relates to the favourable numbers 2, 6 and 8 on the *lo shu* magic square.

POSITION OF THE MALAY HEALER AND PATIENT

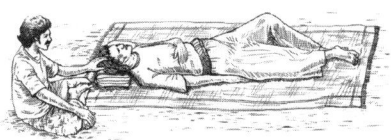

- The patient lies on a mat with his body extending from east to west.
- The healer sits on the right side of the patient, near his head.
- The patient's feet face west. His left side faces south.

Source: *Royal Healer* by Roland Werner, 2002

ARCHITECTURAL SYMBOLISM

Building	Symbol
Menara Maybank	a kris
Menara TM	a bamboo shoot
Tabung Haji Building	the five pillars of Islam
Tun Sambanthan Building	a gopuram (monumental tower at the entrance of a Hindu temple)
National Library	a songket tengkolok (Malay cloth headdress)
National Art Gallery	the gajah menyusu (traditional Malay house design resembling a suckling elephant)
Bintulu Development Authority Building	a tudung saji (food cover)
National Theatre	a sirih junjung (cone-shaped arrangement of betel leaves on a pedestal tray)

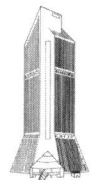
Menara Maybank

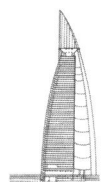
Menara TM

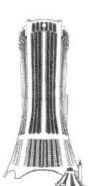
Tabung Haji Building

Tun Sambanthan Building

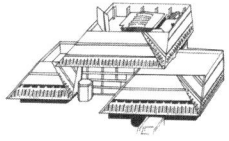
National Library

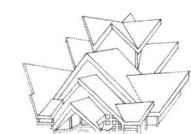
National Theatre

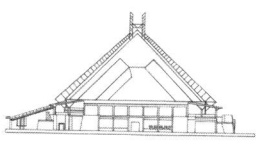
National Art Gallery

Bintulu Development Authority Building

CUTI-CUTI MALAYA, 1932

Itinerary of an inclusive tour through the Federated Malay States from Penang to Singapore.

Day	Place	Arrival and Departure	Time	Conveyance	Remarks
1	Penang	Arrival	—	Steamer	—
	Penang		Morning	Motor car	Drive to Botanic Gardens and Chinese Temple, Ayer Hitam.
			Afternoon	Motor car	Drive around the island.
	Penang	Departure	8 a.m.	Ferry and train	Breakfast on train.
2	Ipoh	Arrival	1.13 p.m.	Train	Station Hotel.
	Ipoh		Afternoon	Motor car	One hour's drive round town, visiting Chinese cave temples on outskirts.
	Ipoh		7 a.m.	Motor car	Drive 10½ miles through picturesque country and rubber estates to Gopeng Tin Mine, returning to hotel for breakfast about 9.30 a.m.
3	Ipoh	Departure	1.23 p.m	Train	Restaurant car on train.
	Kuala Lumpur	Arrival	6.22 p.m	Train	Station Hotel.
	Kuala Lumpur		After breakfast	Motor car	Drive round town, visiting agricultural gardens where growth and preparation of rubber will be demonstrated. The Malay mosque, museum, etc.
4	Kuala Lumpur		Afternoon	Motor car	Drive to Batu Caves and Sungei Besi Tin Mines.
	Kuala Lumpur	Departure	8.30 p.m.	Train (Sleeping cars)	Dinner on train.
5	Singapore	Arrival	8.16 a.m.	Train	—

Source: *British Malaya: General Description of the Country and Life Therein* by the Malayan Information Agency, 1932

IMAGERY PROHIBITED IN NEWSPAPERS AND MAGAZINES

- Naked pictures of men and women.
- Pictures of men wearing only G-strings.
- Pictures of topless men or women wearing clothes revealing part of their breasts.
- Pictures of women wearing only bras and panties.
- Pictures of women wearing bikinis.
- Pictures of women wearing lace or see-through fabric where their private parts are clearly visible.
- Pictures of semi-naked women in alluring poses.
- Pictures of women with their private parts blackened, but still in alluring poses.
- Advertisements for undergarments like bras and panties worn by models or mannequins.
- Excerpts from the Qur'an.
- Advertisements from Israel.
- Advertisements showing pictures of the Ka'abah or a mosque in the background.
- Advertisements for contraceptives.
- Aerial pictures (unless permitted by the Department of Survey and Mapping Malaysia).
- Pictures of spaces in all protected places and protected areas under Ordinance 33/59.
- Pictures of all protected places or areas under Act 88/72.
- Horrifying pictures of real events (like a close up photograph of somebody covered in blood or somebody decapitated in an accident).
- Advertisements from foreign embassies except with the permission of the Ministry of Home Affairs.

Source: Ministry of Home Affairs

THE DINING HABITS OF MALAYSIAN TIGERS

According to experienced wildlife rangers, the meat of choice for Malaysian tigers is wild boar, followed by barking deer. Their diet is supplemented by sambar deer and occasionally primates, mouse deer and porcupines. Interestingly, researchers in Malaysia have no records of tigers eating tapirs, even though the tapir's size makes it an energy-efficient kill and thus, by default, a prime candidate for tiger food.

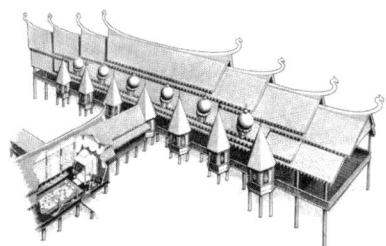

"NO OTHER PLACE IN THE WHOLE WORLD LIKE IT".

A description from the *Sejarah Melayu* (Malay Annals) of the sultan of Malacca's palace, destroyed in 1511 by the invading Portuguese:

"And the size of that palace was seventeen spaces, for each space the breadth was three fathoms, the columns were as large around as could be embraced; of seven levels were the pinnacles. In between that were provided windows, in between those windows were placed roofs at right angles and like suckling elephants, all of them with wings like those of a kite and carved projecting from under the eaves, in between that projection was carried out the 'rectangular grasshopper', all of it with peaks and fringes all over. Moreover all those windows of the palace were altogether painted and gilded with liquid gold, its pinnacles were red glass. When it caught the rays of the sun its form blazed like a jewel; and the walling of that palace was paneled all over, moreover inset with Chinese mirrors of large sizes. When it caught the glare of the sun its form blazed in flashes, so that its image was not clear to peoples' sight. Moreover the crossbeams of that palace were a cubit broad, a hand and two fingers thick; as for the upstand it was two cubits in breadth, a cubit in thickness, the frames of those doors were carved, and forty was the number of those doors, all of them painted and gilded with liquid gold. Exceedingly beautiful was the execution of that palace; there was no other palace in the whole world like it. And that palace it was which was called by men, Mahaligai. Its roof covering was brass and tin crested."

TOO MUCH OF A GOOD THING

In July 1995, Abdul Talib Haron, 35, was found guilty in Johor of 17 offences relating to religious laws, and the fact that he had 10 wives. The self-proclaimed preacher was jailed for 25 months and fined RM14,000. His four lawful wives were jailed a month and fined RM500 each. His six other "wives" were jailed a month and fined RM1,500 each.

SIX MAJOR MEDICALLY CERTIFIED CAUSES OF DEATH, 2020

Disease	Urban	Rural
Heart disease	17.2%	16.5%
Pneumonia	11.3%	11.4%
Cerebrovascular diseases	7.9%	9.2%
Transport accidents	2.7%	3.3%
Chronic lower respiratory diseases	-	2,8%
Malignant neoplasm, trachea, bronchus and lung	2.6%	-

WAXING LYRICAL ABOUT THE DURIAN

"...like eating a sweet raspberry blancmange in a lavatory."
—Anthony Burgess, *Time for a Tiger*

"Sweet, citrusy Silly Putty mixed with onion powder, marinated in spoiled milk."
—Kate Klonick, *Esquire magazine*, July 2007

"A rich custard highly flavoured with almonds gives the best general idea of it, but there are occasional wafts of flavour that call to mind cream-cheese, onion-sauce, sherry-wine, and other incongruous dishes. Then there is a rich glutinous smoothness in the pulp which nothing else possesses, but which adds to its delicacy. It is neither acid nor sweet nor juicy; yet it wants neither of these qualities, for it is in itself perfect. It produces no nausea or other bad effect, and the more you eat of it the less you feel inclined to stop. In fact, to eat durians is a new sensation worth a voyage to the East to experience."
—Alfred Russel Wallace, 19th-century naturalist

"...completely rotten, mushy onions."
—Andrew Zimmer, food writer, dining critic and chef

"Its taste can only be described as...indescribable, something you will either love or despise....Your breath will smell as if you'd been French-kissing your dead grandmother."
—Anthony Bourdain, food critic, author, television host and chef

"...its odor is best described as pig [excrement], turpentine and onions, garnished with a gym sock. It can be smelled from yards away."
—Richard Sterling, travel and food writer

THE FIRST MALAY PROFESSOR

Malaysia's first Malay professor was Ungku Abdul Aziz Ungku Abdul Hamid. At the age of 39, he was appointed the Chair of Economics at Universiti Malaya in 1961. He was awarded the title of Royal Professor in 1978.

MALAYSIA IN SINGAPORE

After Singapore left the Federation of Malaysia in 1965, Keretapi Tanah Melayu (KTM), the main railway operator in Malaysia, continued to operate the railway line into Singapore. As a result, Malaysia had partial sovereignty over the railway tracks and the land on which the Keppel Road Railway Station stood. This arrangement ended in 2011 with the land reverting to Singapore.

MEAN MONTHLY GROSS HOUSEHOLD INCOME, RM

Year	Overall	Bumiputera	Chinese	Indian
1957	207	134	288	228
1967	226	154	329	245
1970	261	172	394	304
1979	417	492	938	746
1984	695	852	1,502	1,094
1987	834	868	1,430	1,089
1990	1,167	940	1,631	1,289
1995	2,020	1,604	2,890	2,140
1997	2,606	2,038	3,738	2,896
1999	2,472	1,984	3,456	2,702
2002	3,011	2,376	4,279	3,044
2004	3,249	2,711	4,437	3,456
2019	7,901	7,090	9,900	8,220

Source: Department of Statistics Malaysia

SOME FOREIGN FILMS SHOT IN MALAYSIA

English Films	Stars	Location
Three Came Home (1950)	Claudette Colbert, Patric Knowles	Sandakan, Sabah
South Pacific (1958)	Rossano Brazzi, Mitzi Gaynor	Pulau Tioman, Johor
Paper Tiger (1975)	David Niven, Toshiro Mifune	Genting Highlands, Pahang
Bat 21 (1988)	Gene Hackman, Danny Glover	Sabah
Farewell to the King (1989)	Nick Nolte, Nigel Havers	Sarawak
Anna and the King (1999)	Chow Yun-Fatt, Jodie Foster	Penang, Langkawi, Perak
Entrapment (1999)	Sean Connery, Catherine Zeta Jones	Kuala Lumpur
The Sleeping Dictionary (2001)	Jessica Alba, Bob Hoskins	Sarawak
The Touch (2002)	Michelle Yeoh, Ben Chaplin	Penang
Marco Polo (2014)	Lorenzo Richelmy, Benedict Wong	Johor Bahru

Chinese Films	Stars	Location
Police Story 3 (1992)	Jackie Chan, Michelle Yeoh	Kuala Lumpur
Summer Holiday (2000)	Sammi Cheng, Richie Ren	Terengganu (Pulau Redang), Malacca
Skyline Cruisers (2000)	Leon Lai Ming, Jordan Chan, Shu Qi	Perak, Kuala Lumpur, Tang Wei
Looking for Mr Perfect (2003)	Shu Qi, Andy On	Kuala Lumpur
Lust, Caution (2006)	Tony Leung Chiu-Wai, Tang Wei	Perak, Penang
After This Our Exile (2006)	Aaron Kwok, Gouw Ian Iskandar, Charlie Yeung	Perak (Ipoh, Teluk Intan)

Indian Films	Stars	Location
One 2 Ka 4 (2001)	Shahrukh Khan, Juhi Chawla	Malacca
Hum Kisi Se Kam Nahin (2002)	Amitabh Bachchan, Sanjay Dutt	Kuala Lumpur
Don (2006)	Shahrukh Khan, Priyanka Chopra, Arjun Rampal	Kuala Lumpur, Langkawi
Billa (2007)	Ajith Kumar, Prabhu Ganesan	Kuala Lumpur, Langkawi
Kuruvi (2008)	Vijay, Trisha Krishnan	Kuala Lumpur

LAKSA: A SPICY MALAYSIAN SOUP

Laksa Perlis and Laksa Kedah
Distinguishing ingredients: Sliced boiled eggs and eel flesh.

Laksa Penang or Asam Laksa
Distinguishing ingredients: Mackerel, tamarind, pineapple, mint leaves.

Laksa Kelantan, or Lakse
Distinguishing ingredients: Creamy white coconut milk gravy, white noodles.

Laksa Kuala Kangsar
Distinguishing ingredients: Hand-made noodles, light gravy.

Laksam (Terengganu)
Distinguishing ingredients: Thick, flat, white rice flour noodles, white gravy of boiled fish and coconut milk.

Laksa Ipoh
Distinguishing ingredient: Prawn paste.

Laksa Johor
Distinguishing ingredients: Dried prawns, beansprouts, spaghetti-like rice noodles and sweet, light gravy.

Curry Laksa (Selangor)
Distinguishing ingredients: Thick coconut gravy, deep fried tofu, cockles, long beans.

Laksa Nyonya (Malacca)
Distinguishing ingredients: Belacan (shrimp paste), lime, cockles, fresh prawns, rich coconut gravy.

Laksa Sarawak
Distinguishing ingredients: Chicken slices, sliced omelette, prawns, beansprouts, Sarawak laksa paste, vermicelli.

0   125 km

Height in metres of the flagpole in Merdeka Square, Kuala Lumpur:

THE WORLD'S LARGEST FLOWER

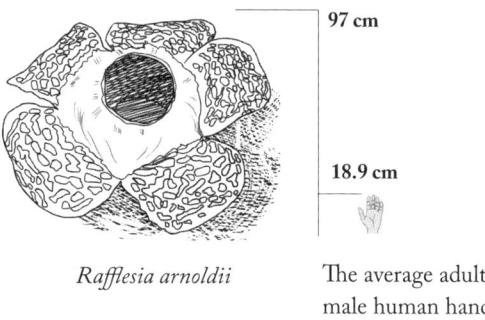

Rafflesia arnoldii   The average adult male human hand

BLOOMING PHASES OF THE RAFFLESIA

1. Rafflesia buds develop from minute strands spread through the host tree or vine's stem tissues.
2. The Rafflesia bud breaks through the host's bark.
3. Nine months later, the mature bud is the size of a small cabbage.
4. The putrid-smelling open bloom lasts only from two to five days.

CARS IN MALAYSIAN MUSEUMS

The National Automobile Museum in Sepang but there are three cars in other museums in Malaysia of particular interest.

The Rolls-Royce in which Sir Henry Gurney was travelling when he was ambushed and killed in 1951 is at the Penang Museum.

The first Proton Saga to be produced in 1983 is at the Muzium Negara, Kuala Lumpur.

Visitors to the Petroleum Museum in Miri, can sit in a Perodua car, and with different settings, can experience what it would be like if there were different levels of earthquakes.

HOW TO BE INITIATED INTO A TRIAD IN 19TH-CENTURY MALAYA

1. Go to a designated clearing in a jungle, estate or Chinese graveyard after nightfall. The area will be lit by flickering candles, marked out with sticks and strings, decorated by hanging strips of red paper with Chinese characters written on them and an altar table on which will sit a bowl filled with rice with a ruler, scissors, mirror or sword as well as coloured paper flags and joss sticks standing in it.

2. While the leader of the triad is chanting ritual verses, invoking the spirits of the society's ancestors, and the other members are entering and standing around the designated area, you must wait patiently with the rest of the initiates or "new horses" outside and watch and listen.

3. Remove your shoes and jacket. Discard all metal articles such as jewellery and belt buckles. Roll up the sleeve of your shirt so that your shoulder is bared. Along with the other initiates, tie a white cloth around your head.

4. Walk around the designated area counter-clockwise until you reach an opening. You will be stopped and interrogated by two guardian members of the triad. Reply to their questions and demonstrate your knowledge of the triad.

5. After successfully answering the queries, proceed into the designated area with your head bowed, holding a lighted joss stick. When you are approached from behind by another guardian member, who will place a *parang* (machete) on the back of your neck, declare your loyalty to the triad and swear secrecy.

6. Approach the altar. Along with the other initiates, prick your left middle finger with a needle and let the blood drip into a bowl. Chant a prayer.

7. After a white chicken (symbolising a traitor) is sacrificed, cross your arms and, holding a *parang*, touch the animal's corpse while swearing loyalty and secrecy.

8. Listen while the leader reads out the "36 oaths", prescribing the triad's prohibitions (for example, adultery with the wife or sister of another member, refusing to help another member in a fight, and introducing a government officer as a candidate for triad membership) and punishments (for example, "eating the vermicelli" (being tied up with ropes), "death by bath" (being tied up in a sack and drowned) and "death by knives").

9. When the bowl of blood, balanced on a *parang*, is passed around, take a sip of the blood and swear again your secrecy and loyalty to the triad.

10. Receive your diploma: a piece of red paper on which is written your name, the names of the other members present at the ceremony as well as a number of composite Chinese characters which, when deciphered, form a secret phrase.

Source: Adapted from *The Impact of Chinese Secret Societies in Malaya* by Wilfred Blythe, 1969

SOME OF THE COUNTRY'S OLDEST REGISTERED COMPANIES

Name of company	Current location	Date of registration / incorporation	Type of business
Scopal Company Ltd	Johor Bahru, Johor	1900	Housing development
Proctor & Gamble (Malaysia) Sdn Bhd	Petaling Jaya, Selangor	1900	Cosmetic and personal care products
Tan Chee Seng Sawmill Sdn Bhd	Ipoh, Perak	1900	Timber processing
Mardec Berhad (formerly known as the Malaysian Rubber Development Corporation)	Ampang, Selangor	1900	Rubber and polymer processing, trading and manufacturing
Pan Malaysian Wood Berhad	Ipoh, Perak	1900	Manufacturing plywood, fibrewood, particleboard
Kim Lian Huat Sawmills Sdn Bhd	Klang, Selangor	1900	Petroleum supplier
Tong Hing Holdings Sdn Bhd	Inanam, Sabah	1900	Wine industry
ABN Amro Bank N.V.	Penang	1900	Finance
The Bombay Burmah Trading Corporation Ltd	Johor Bahru, Johor	1900	Trade and investment
Hiap Thye Shipbuilding Industry Berhad	Sibu, Sarawak	1900	Shipbuilding and repair
Boon Siew (Borneo) Sendirian Berhad	Inanam, Sabah	1900	Sale of motorcycles and other motor vehicles, motor oils
Samarahan Plantations Sdn Bhd	Serian, Sarawak	1900	Oil palm plantation
Sabah Shell Petroleum Company Limited	Kota Kinabalu, Sabah	1900	Oil and gas production
Guan Chow Sdn Bhd	Ipoh, Perak	1900	Sale of bicycles and bicycle parts
Johore Shipping Sdn Bhd	Port Klang, Selangor	1900	Water transport support system
Bertam Consolidated Rubber Company Ltd	Georgetown, Penang	1904	Palm oil manufacturing
The Kampong Kuantan Rubber Co. Ltd	Kuala Lumpur	1904	Plantation management
The Pataling Rubber Estates Ltd	Kuala Lumpur	1906	Agriculture, forestry
Rahman Hydraulic Tin Sdn Bhd	Klian Intan, Perak	1907	Mining
Inova Pharmaceuticals (Singapore) Pte Ltd	Shah Alam, Selangor	1907	Medical equipment supplier
The Ayer Molek Rubber Company Bhd	Kuala Lumpur	1909	Rubber estates

Source: Suruhanjaya Syarikat Malaysia

THE DINING HABITS OF SEA SNAILS: SUCKING IT UP

Oyster drills are sea snails found in Malaysian waters which prey on oysters by drilling a small hole through the oyster shells using a rasping device known as a radula. The snail's proboscis is inserted through the hole into the oyster's flesh and the meat is then sucked into the drill's stomach.

Other species of sea snails are known to make small cuts on the surface of larger sea creatures, such as rays, inserting their proboscises into the wounds and sucking the blood of the animal. They are also known to insert their proboscises into the mouth, gill slits and anus of their prey.

THE SCALE OF THINGS

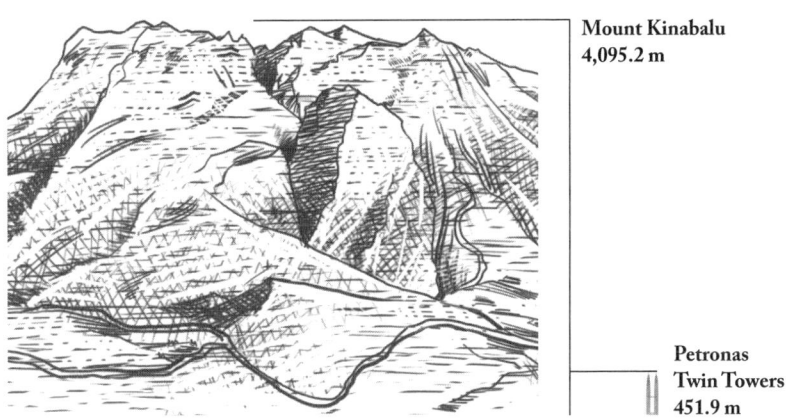

Mount Kinabalu
4,095.2 m

Petronas
Twin Towers
451.9 m

USES OF A SARONG

- silat weapon
- turban
- tablecloth
- blanket
- sack for carrying items, especially dry food

- clothing for men (sampin)
- clothing for women (headscarf or dress)
- baby cradle, baby carrier or swing
- shroud to cover a dead body
- towel

The collective age of the three oldest female elephants (Limba, Miss Rocco and Girl) in the Kota Kinabalu Zoo:

THE FIRST CITIZENSHIP CERTIFICATE HOLDER

The first Malayan citizenship certificate holder was 17-year-old Kok Shoo Yin, who received his document on 14 November 1957.

Source: *New Straits Times*

TYPES OF DIVORCE IN ISLAM

Talaq	Unilateral pronouncement by the husband; he says the word "*talaq*" three times.
Fasakh	Dissolution of marriage by a court on certain grounds such as abuse or neglect.
Ta'liq	Dissolution of marriage by a court due to a breach of the marital contract.
Khuluq	Divorce by redemption; the wife pays the husband to release her.

MORTALITY RATES PER 1,000 PERSONS BY STATE, 2020

State	Neonatal mortality rate	Infant mortality rate	Toddler mortality rate	Maternal mortality rate	Crude death rate
Johor	4.2	6.9	0.4	0.2	6.7
Kedah	4.7	7.4	0.5	0.5	8.6
Kelantan	3.3	7.9	0.8	0.4	7.7
Malacca	5.4	9.0	0.5	0.1	7.1
Negeri Sembilan	3.3	5.9	0.4	0.4	7.6
Pahang	4.8	9.3	0.8	0.4	6.5
Perak	4.1	7.8	0.6	0.2	8.5
Perlis	4.3	6.8	0.3	0.5	7.8
Penang	5.1	8.1	0.4	0.2	8.0
Sabah	1.1	2.3	0.2	0.2	5.5
Sarawak	3.2	5.4	0.4	0.2	7.1
Selangor	3.4	5.7	0.4	0.2	6.0
Terengganu	6.0	9.6	0.6	0.3	7.2
Kuala Lumpur	2.8	4.8	0.3	0.2	6.8
Labuan	6.0	8.0	0.4	0.0	5.4
Putrajaya	-	-	-	-	2.3
Malaysia	3.7	6.5	0.4	0.3	4.5

Source: Ministry of Health Malaysia

P. RAMLEE TRIVIA

Aristocracy	P. Ramlee's birth name was Teuku Zakaria. Teuku is an Acehnese aristocratic title.
P	The "P" in P. Ramlee's name stands for "Puteh", short for Teuku Nyak Puteh, which is actually his father's name. His father was a sailor from Lho' Seumawe, Aceh, who migrated to Penang.
A star is born	P. Ramlee wrote a song called Azizah and performed his original composition at an agricultural festival in Penang in 1948. The song, which was about his love interest in Penang, became his first hit song.
First film	As an actor, P. Ramlee's first film was Chinta (Love) in 1948, directed by Tamil film director B.S. Rajhans. His first leading role came in the 1950 film Bakti (Deeds). In 1955, P. Ramlee directed his first film, Penarik Becha (The Trishaw Man).
Colour film	P. Ramlee's only colour film was Hang Tuah (1956). Based on the legendary Malay warrior, the film was directed by Indian director Phani Majumdar.
Influences	P. Ramlee drew influences from many sources: – Penarik Becha (Trishaw Man, 1955) was based on a Japanese film entitled Rickshaw-san. – Bujang Lapok (Three Raggedy Bachelors, 1955) and the Do Re Mi series were based on The Three Stooges. – Kancan Tirana (1969) was adapted from Akira Kurosawa's Sanshiro Sugata. – Damaq in "Ragam P. Ramlee" (1965) was adapted from Hollywood's Love Me Tender. – Madu Tiga (Three Wives, 1964) was adapted from a Chinese film. – Penarik Becha and Semerah Padi (Village of Semerah Padi, 1956) bore similarities to the cinematographic styles of Satyajit Ray and Akira Kurosawa.
International acclaim	American artiste Lobo re-recorded P. Ramlee's song Getaran Jiwa (The Stirring of My Soul) as Whispers in the Wind on his 1995 Classic Hits album. Additionally, P. Ramlee's song Jeritan Batinku (The Cry of My Soul) was re-recorded in English by Kiko Shimada of Japan and retitled Indian Summer. The Bolshoi Ballet Theatre of Tashkent has also recorded an album comprising P. Ramlee compositions.
Recipe for a good voice	P. Ramlee advised singers to eat a lot of fruit (but avoid consuming sticky fruits), to maintain a healthy lifestyle, and to train their voices.
Coining a new word	P. Ramlee coined the word pawagam (cinema), an abbreviated form of panggung wayang gambar or "motion picture theatre".
Last film	P. Ramlee's final film was Laksamana Do Re Mi (Admirals Do, Re and Mi) in 1972.
Swan song	P. Ramlee's final song before his death in 1973 was Ayer Mata di Kuala Lumpur (Tears in Kuala Lumpur). The song spoke of the artiste's failed ambitions after he moved from Singapore to Kuala Lumpur.

BETEL-CHEWING TRADITIONS

"In [a] visit with the King [of Kedah]... he honours the guest with a seat near him and will chew a little betel and spit it out on [a] little gold saucer and sends it by page to the guest who must take it with all signs of humility and satisfaction and chew it after him; very dangerous to refuse royal morsel."
—Captain Alexander Hamilton, 1727

STDS IN THE COLONY

Ethnicity of women from whom European men, treated at the Sultan Street Clinic in Kuala Lumpur, contracted venereal disease (per cent).

	1927	1928	1930	1931
Chinese	12.8	19.8	23.6	27.6
Malays	55.2	43.5	28.7	30.3
Siamese	6.1	14.3	31.5	36.0
Tamils	12.3	13.5	5.6	3.1
Japanese	8.4	6.3	4.6	0.4
Eurasians	–	2.3	1.4	0.4
Europeans	–	–	–	2.2
Others	5.0	–	4.6	–
No. of cases	179	237	216	228

Source: Annual Reports of the FMS Medical Department

GOAT-BREEDING TIPS

Stud goats at the National Boer Goat Breeding Centre in Pondok Tanjung, Perak, which can "service" up to 80 females goats, are typically given a week's rest after each phase of exertion and fed with *tongkat ali* (a local aphrodisiac), eggs and honey.

Source: Based on account before the national parliament given by Deputy Agriculture and Agro-Based Industry Minister Datuk Rohani Abdul Karim. She also stated, "I call the stud a hero."

MALAYSIAN FOOD CALORIE COUNTER

Food Item	Calories
Capati (1 piece) served with green gravy	376
Cekodok pisang (1 piece)	179
Chicken curry (1 medium piece)	195
Chicken rice (1 plate)	278
Chicken satay (5 sticks)	100
Coconut flesh (1 cup)	283
Curry puff (1 piece)	129
Dodol (1 piece)	71
Durian (6 pieces)	357
Fried chicken (1 piece)	255
Fried ikan kembong (1 piece)	111
Fried kuey teow (1 plate)	321
Fried meehoon (1 plate)	294
Guava (1 small slice)	41
Ikan bilis sambal (2 tbsp)	252
Kangkung belacan (4 tbsp)	96
Kesari (1 medium piece)	172
Kuih appam balik (1 piece)	245
Kuih koci pulut hitam (1 piece)	180
Kuih pau kacang merah (1 small piece)	34

Food Item	Calories
Kuih seri muka (1 piece)	144
Mango (1 medium)	226
Mata kucing (10 whole, small)	29
Mee bandung (1 bowl)	549
Mee curry (1 bowl)	529
Mee goreng (1 plate)	281
Mee soup (1 bowl)	383
Nasi briyani (1 plate)	224
Nasi dagang (1 plate)	508
Nasi goreng (1 plate)	637
Nasi lemak (1 plate)	389
Papaya (1 small slice)	56
Pineapple tart (1 piece)	15
Pisang goreng (1 piece)	117
Popiah (1 piece)	94
Red bean porridge with coconut milk (1 bowl)	101
Rojak (4 tbsp)	182
Roti canai (1 piece) with dhal	332
Roti telur (1 piece)	356
Teh tarik (1 cup)	83
Wajik (1 piece)	65

Source: Amway

MALAYSIA'S TANGIBLE NATIONAL HERITAGE

As declared in the National Heritage Act 2005 (Act 645), Part VI, Section 23(1):

Heritage sites
- Batu Caves, Selangor
- Bukit Jawa, Perak (Tool workshop from 100,000 to 200,000 years ago)
- Carcosa and Seri Negara, Kuala Lumpur (1896/1900)
- Christ Church, Malacca (1741)
- Dewan Bandaraya and Panggung Bandaraya Building, Kuala Lumpur (1896)
- General Post Office building, Kuala Lumpur (1904)
- Gunung Runtuh Cave, Perak (54,000 years ago)
- Istana Negara (National Palace; 1928)
- Jabatan Kerja Raya (Public Works Department) Building, Kuala Lumpur (1905)
- Kinabalu National Park, Sabah
- Kota Tampan, Perak (Tool workshop from around 74,000 years ago)
- Kuala Lumpur Railway Station (1892)
- Masjid Jamek, Kuala Lumpur (1909)
- Masjid Kampung Hulu, Malacca (1728)
- • Masjid Kampung Kling, Malacca (1748)
- Merdeka Square, Kuala Lumpur (1957)
- Merdeka Stadium, Kuala Lumpur (1956)
- Mulu National Park, Sarawak
- National Monument, Kuala Lumpur (1966)
- National Mosque and Warriors' Mausoleum, Kuala Lumpur (1963)
- National Museum, Kuala Lumpur (1962)
- Old Palace and Royal Museum, Negeri Sembilan (1902)
- Parliament House, Kuala Lumpur (1962)
- Perak Museum, Taiping (1883)
- Railways (KTMB) Headquarters, Kuala Lumpur (1917)
- Residency Building, Kuala Lumpur (1888)
- Selangor Chinese Assembly Hall, Kuala Lumpur (1910)
- Sri Poyyatha Vinayagar Moorthi Temple, Malacca (1781)
- St. George's Church, Penang (1818)
- Stadthuys, Malacca (1650)
- Sultan Abdul Samad Building (1897)
- Sultan Idris Teaching College / University, Perak (1919)
- Universiti Malaya (UM), Kuala Lumpur (1962)
- Victoria Institution, Kuala Lumpur (1893)

Heritage Objects
- Bronze Bell, Johor (15 CE)
- Bunga Raya (*Hibiscus rosa-sinensis*)
- Cogan Agama (Royal sceptre of religion)
- Cogan Alam (Royal sceptre of the universe)
- Cokmar (Royal maces)
- Cokmar Dewan Negara (Senate mace)
- Cokmar Dewan Rakyat (House of Representatives mace)
- Declaration of Independence
- Fish cooked in clay, Perlis
- Gandik Diraja (Royal tiara)
- Golden Coin of Sultan Alau'uddin Riayat Shah II of Johor (1528–1564)
- Golden Coin of Sultan Muzaffar Shah of Johor (1564–1570)
- Golden Coin of Sultan Zainal Abidin II of Terengganu (1793–1808)
- Hikayat Hang Tuah manuscript
- Hukum Kanun Malacca (Laws of Malacca)
- Jalur Gemilang (the Malaysian flag)
- Jata Negara (Malaysian national emblem)
- Kalung Diraja (Royal necklace)
- Keris Panjang Diraja (Royal long keris)
- Keris Pendek Diraja (Royal short keris)
- Kijang Emas bullion gold coin
- Letters of Sultan Abdul Hamid (1882–1943)
- Panji-panji Diraja (Royal flag)
- Pending Diraja (Royal belt buckle)
- Pending Melayu, Kelantan (Malay belt buckle)
- Perak Man (skeletal remains of a man who lived 10,000 years ago)
- Royal Tobacco Box of Terengganu (c. 1800s)
- Sculpture of Seated Buddha, Bujang Valley, Kedah (1000–1100 CE)

- Sejarah Melayu (Malay Annals) manuscript
- Statue of Avalokitesvara, Perak (7th and 12th centuries CE)
- Stone axes in suevite, Perak (more than 1.8 million years old)
- Tengkolok Diraja (Royal headdress)
- Tepak Sireh (Betel quid set) of Sultan Abdul Samad (1859–1880)

Paintings
- *As Night Begins* by Tan Tiong Yeo (1950s)
- *Batu Serlin–Pahang River* by Frank Swettenham, (1885)
- *Boatman on Pahang River* by George Giles (1885)
- *Bumi Yang Bahagia Lombong Bijih Timah Malaya* by Abdullah Ariff (1960)
- *Che Ali* by George Giles (1885)
- Conversation by Yong Mun Sen (1941)
- *Fishing Village* by Chung Chen Sun (1958)
- *Landscape* by Ab Ibrahim (1940)
- *Lembu Berlaga* by Tay Hooi Keat (1958)
- *Mandi Laut* by Datuk Syed Ahmad Jamal (1957)
- *Market Place Telubin & Fish Market* by William Samwell (1893)
- *Mencelop Batik* by Cheong Lai Tong (1958)
- *Minah* by Datuk Mohd Hoessien Enas (1958)
- *My Wife in Her Wedding Dress* by O. Don Peris (1933)
- *On The Taiping Hill* by Frank Swettenham (1884)
- *Perak River From The Residency Kuala Kangsar* by Frank Swettenham (1884)
- *Perayaan Pulau Pinang* by Chuah Thean Teng (1952)
- *Raft Boatman on Pahang River* by George Giles (1885)
- *River Pergau State of Kelantan* by William Samwell (1893)
- *Spirit of Earth, Water and Air* by Patrick Ng Kah Onn (1958)
- *Swettenham on Raft Leaving Permatang Tinggi* by George Giles (1885)
- *The Great Office That Stands on Kangsar's Hill* by Frank Swettenham (1884)

Living Heritage
- Haji Abu Bakar Jaafar (Boria entertainer)
- Haji Ali Badron Haji Sabo (storyteller)
- Losimin Majanil (Kadazan Dusun female shaman)
- Mohd Bahroodin Ahmad (Bangsawan, Boria and Ronggeng entertainer)
- Tan Hooi Song (traditional drummer)
- Vatsala G.R. Kurup (Bharatanatyam dancer, choreographer, artistic director)

Source: National Heritage Department

SHOOT ON SIGHT

Crows were first brought to Malaya at the end of the 19th century to control caterpillar outbreaks on coffee estates near Klang. They have flourished, and are culled periodically by shooting parties sent out by the local councils.

In 1974, the Sultan of Selangor ordered that the crows in Klang not be harmed. Officials organised an audio blitz—the blare and blast of loudspeakers drove the crows to the river where they were shepherded upriver by boats armed with more loudspeakers and officers firing guns into the air.

The birds apparently did not appreciate the noisy farewell ceremony. Klang and other towns are still infested with crows. Culling still takes place.

NUMBER OF FIRE BREAKOUTS BY SOURCE, 2007

Non-incendiary arson	4,994
Electricity	4,021
Source unknown	3,174
Others	2,372
Cigarette butts	1,558
Incendiary arson	1,157
Gas, kerosene stove	1,138
Sparks of fire	667
Mosquito coil, candle, torch	400
Spontaneous reaction	385
Children playing with matches	253
Firecrackers/fireworks	69
Chemical reaction	37
Total	**20,225**

Source: Fire and Rescue Department Malaysia

MEDICAL MALPRACTICE

When an 11-year-old boy accidentally sliced off the tip of his left index finger while chopping off the top of a coconut with a *parang* in 2007, his mother rushed him to the Sultanah Bahiyah Hospital in Sungai Petani. She carefully packed the severed fingertip in ice, hoping that the doctors would be able to reattach it. However, one of the hospital staff took the fingertip and, after deciding it could not be reattached, flushed it down the toilet. The mother lodged a police report at the Alor Star police station.

⁎ ⁎ ⁎

In 2007, police in Kuala Lumpur arrested an unidentified 63-year-old man who had been practising as a dentist for 29 years, although he had no medical training. He treated patients at his home in an enormous 1940s examining chair, which had been cast off by the Malaysian army in 1978. The man's closest brush with the dental profession came in the 1960s when he assisted an army dentist by carrying his bag on visits to plantation workers' homes. He was charged with illegally practising dentistry.

Source: *New Straits Times*, Reuters

FAMOUS AND INFAMOUS GOVERNMENT "OPERATIONS"

Operation Matador was a plan of the British Malaya Command to launch a pre-emptive strike into Thailand in 1941 to prevent Japanese soldiers landing in Thailand and then invading northern Malaya. The British delayed launching Matador and it failed.

Operation Good Citizen was a campaign launched by the government in 1967 to foster a deeper sense of national pride and patriotism, to inculcate a greater respect for national symbols including the flag and anthem, and to promote an active feeling of civic consciousness and cooperation among Malaysian citizens and residents.

Operation Swop, initiated by the Malaysian government in 1968 after Singapore's decision to revoke non-citizen work permits, aimed to replace 60,000 Singaporean workers in Kuala Lumpur with Malaysian workers.

Operation Hair was a campaign launched by the Selangor Education Department in 1972 to ensure that students and teachers did not sport long hair that was "painful to the eye". Barbers were called to schools to give on-the-spot haircuts.

Operation Judas was a massive campaign by Malaysian law enforcement authorities in 1973 to detain individuals who were allegedly collaborating with communist terrorists.

Operasi Buaya Ganas (violent crocodile) was a concerted effort on the part of the authorities and residents of Sarawak in 1982 to curb the increasing number of crocodile attacks that had been occurring by hunting and killing the reptiles.

Operation Lalang (weeding) was carried out in 1987 by the police and Special Branch to crack down on opposition leaders and social activists. The operation saw the arrest of 106 persons under the Internal Security Act (ISA) and the revoking of the publishing licences of two daily newspapers, *The Star* and the *Sin Chew Jit Poh* and two weeklies, *The Sunday Star* and *Watan*. The Prime Minister Dato' Seri Dr Mahathir Mohamad said the operation was necessary to defuse racial tensions which had reached "dangerous proportions".

Operation Nyah (get away) is an ongoing operation launched by government authorities in Sabah in 1992 to round up and deport illegal immigrants in the country and prevent other illegal immigrants from entering Malaysia.

Operation Sikap (attitude) is an ongoing traffic safety operation launched in 2001 by the Royal Malaysian Police to ensure safety on all roads in Malaysia during festive seasons.

Operation Valentine was aimed at curbing *khalwat* (close proximity) violations between unmarried Muslims. Islamic religious authorities in Kuantan, Pahang arrested 26 unmarried Muslim couples in hotel rooms on 15 February 2009 during Operation Valentine.

Operation Zipper was a plan to capture parts of Japanese-held Malaya in preparation for Operation Mailfist which was to liberate Singapore. With the ending of World War II, this operation was no longer needed.

SOME NOTABLE QUOTES FROM TUN DR MAHATHIR MOHAMAD

"We have a saying in our part of the world that when two elephants fight, it is the grass that gets trampled. We have a vital interest in ensuring that we do not get trampled and that the two elephants, who are both good friends of ours, do not fight. There is a further twist to this elephant analogy, however. Not only does the grass get trampled when elephants fight, it gets squashed when the elephants sit down to make love." —1985

"I am perhaps the only dictator who has to stand for elections before dictating." —1998

"Currency trading is unnecessary, unproductive and totally immoral." —1998

"Exploit us, but exploit us fairly." —2003

"It is good governance by good people that we need. And feudal kings, even dictators, have provided and can provide good governance." —2005

"My fear is that if people fail to think and criticise that which is wrong, then society will rot." —2005

"People should know the whole truth and nothing but the truth." —2005

"I think this [Malaysia] is a half-past-six country with no guts." —2006

"Treat your opponents like insects. Knock them down and crush them with your feet." (Advice to the Malaysian Thomas Cup badminton team) —2006

SOME FEATURES OF MANGLISH GRAMMAR

1. Dropping the auxiliary verb when forming a question.

   Malaysian English
   "Why you need to know?"
   "What time you coming?"

   Standard English
   "Why do you need to know?"
   "What time are you coming?"

2. Dropping the subject and auxiliary verb when forming a question.

   Malaysian English
   "Eat already?"
   "Why not working today?"

   Standard English
   "Have you already eaten?"
   "Why are you not working today?"

3. Dropping the subject and auxiliary verb and adding the tag "or not" when forming a question.

   Malaysian English
   "Can or not?"
   "Finished or not?"

   Standard English
   "Can you do it?"
   "Have you finished?"

4. Dropping the subject and/or auxiliary verb and adding the particle "ah" to signify a question.

   Malaysian English
   "Borrow your pencil ah?"
   "Nice ah that lady?"

   Standard English
   "Can I borrow your pencil?"
   "Is that lady nice?"

5. Adding the tag "isn't it" to a question to signal a request for a confirmation.

   Malaysian English
   "She dyed her hair red, isn't it?"
   "He went to Australia, isn't it?"

   Standard English
   "She dyed her hair red, didn't she?"
   "Hasn't he gone to Australia?"

6. Using "got" in place of "have" or "there is/are".

   Malaysian English
   "This place got a lot of restaurants."
   "Got prawns in the soup."

   Standard English
   "This place has a lot of restaurants."
   "There are prawns in the soup."

7. Adding the tag "what" to the end of a sentence to express exclamation.

   Malaysian English
   "I didn't steal it what!"
   "Crazy what!"

   Standard English
   "I didn't steal it."
   "This is crazy!"

Source: Adapted from *Language Choices and Discourse of Malaysian Families*, edited by Maya Khemlani, 2006

WINE PAIRINGS

Most people are probably unaware that Malay food can be successfully paired with wines. Here are some examples:

Malay dishes	Suggested wines
Cucur udang (prawn fritters), *popiah goreng* (fried spring rolls), *tauhu sumbat* (stuffed tofu) and *kepak ayam* (chicken wings)	Medium dry white wines which are crisp, with a fruity structure and a well-balanced taste such as a blend of Tempranilo and Cabernet Sauvignon as well as Chardonnay
Otak-otak (Steamed seafood mousse on *kaduk* leaf)	Medium-bodied wines which are structured with a fruity aroma, such as Tempranilo and Cabernet Rose
Sup Ikan Merah (Fillet of red snapper simmered in a lightly spiced fish broth with diced tomatoes and local celery)	Medium-bodied wines with a fruity aftertaste, such as Chardonnay and Pinot Bianco. Also good with Cabernet Rosé
Rusuk Panggang (Chargrilled marinated beef short ribs served with *pegedil*, sweet soy sauce and *sambal belacan*)	Full-bodied wines, with an integrated bouquet of mixed berries and smoky oak with a long, intense finish such as Cabernet Sauvignon Shiraz Merlot
Ayam Kampung Limau Purut (Locally-raised organic chicken simmered in a spicy gravy of chillies, turmeric, kaffir lime and coconut milk)	Fruity sweet wines, which balance the crispness and dryness of the wine, such as Dolcetto, Garnacha Syrah and Cabernet Sauvignon
Masak Lemak Ikan dengan Belimbing (Rich curry of fish simmered in coconut milk with chillies, turmeric and sour carambola)	Fruit-driven palate wines with excellent texture and balance such as Sauvignon Blanc and Chianti Classico Rosso. Also goes well with Rosé
Kari Udang Galah (King prawns cooked in a rich curry of spices and coconut milk)	Full-bodied wines which are fruity sweet and with excellent texture and balance such as Cabernet Shiraz Merlot, Barossa Riesling, Sauvignon Blanc, and Pinot Grigio
Gula Melaka cake with coconut ice cream (Steamed palm sugar sponge cake served with caramelised palm sugar syrup)	Any sweet dessert wines or any medium-bodied wines which exhibit fruity aromas with a long, generous and clean acid thrust finish such as those from the Riesling and Eiswein grape varieties
Chocolate Durian Cake Coconut Crème Caramel	Wines with intense, fruity aroma, rich and refreshing taste such as Cabernet Rose, Pinot Grigio and wines from the Riesling variety

Source: Bijan Restaurant, Kuala Lumpur

THE COST OF DYING

A one-night, Buddhist or Taoist funeral service and cremation package at the Xiao En Centre of the Nilai Memorial Park in Negeri Sembilan costs RM10,888 and includes the following:

- Death or burial certificate
- Body claim and transportation
- Dry ice and make-up services
- Quality certified cremation casket
- Quality urn
- Cremation and ashes pick-up services
- Traditional longevity costume or coat
- Red and white blanket
- Sealing of casket
- Death notice
- Parlour hall
- Photo enlargement and flowered photo frame
- Decorated memorial altar

- Mourning uniform
- Joss sticks and candles
- Two night care personnel (for 1 night, 6 p.m.–12 a.m.)
- Road sign
- Lanterns
- Red packets with sweets
- Offerings to the deceased (fruits and vegetables)
- Drinking water in cups
- Peanuts
- Plastic fan and towel souvenirs
- Condolence book and box
- Toyota Estima hearse or equivalent

Source: Nilai Memorial Park

MALAYSIAN TIME

Period in use	Time offset from GMT	Name of time (unofficial)
1874 – 31 May 1905	+ 6 hr 46 m 48 s	British Malayan Mean Time
1 June 1905 – 31 December 1932	+ 7 hr 00 m 00 s	Standard Zone Time
1 January 1933 – 31 August 1941	+ 7 hr 20 m 00 s	Daylight saving time
1 September 1941 – 15 February 1942	+ 7 hr 30 m 00 s	Daylight saving time
16 February 1942 – 12 September 1945	+ 9 hr 00 m 00 s	Tokyo Standard Time
13 September 1945 – 31 December 1981	+ 7 hr 30 m 00 s	Daylight saving time/ Malaysian Standard Time (Peninsular Malaysia only)
1 January 1982 – Present	+ 8 hr 00 m 00 s	Malaysian Standard Time

Cost in USD millions of the Jusco Bukit Tinggi, the third largest AEON Jusco mall in Asia:

TRADITIONAL MALAY INSULTS

Malay	Translation	Meaning
Hidung belang/ buaya darat.	Striped nosed/land crocodile.	A playboy.
Umpama anjing makan muntahnya.	A dog that eats what it has vomited.	A stingy, miserly person.
Lidah bercabang bagai biawak.	A forked tongue like that of a monitor lizard.	An insincere, treacherous person.
Gajah seekor gembala dua.	An elephant with two mahouts.	A woman with two lovers.
Puteri lilin.	Wax princess.	Someone who can't stand being out in the sun.
Buruk siku.	Bad-elbowed.	Indian giver.
Loncat-loncat bagai ulat pinang.	Hopping about like a betel nut worm.	A restless person.
Lesung mencari alu.	A mortar that seeks the pestle.	A loose woman.
Kaki bangku.	Bench-legged.	Someone who cannot play ball games.
Perempuan itu langkah ular tida lepas.	If that woman treads on a snake she will not escape.	A very ugly woman.
Seperti pikat kehilangan mata.	Like a horse fly that has lost its eyes.	A clumsy, blundering person.
Sudah berjanggut tiada berjubah.	A man who has the beard but not the robe.	An imposter or fraud.

REEL HISTORY

The first Malayan film was *Laila Majnun* in 1933. The inspiration for the film was a classic Persian tale of two doomed lovers. The director, B.S. Rajhans, recruited his cast from a *bangsawan* (Malay opera) troupe. It was produced for the Motilal Chemical Company of Bombay (based in Singapore) by its owner, K.R.S. Christy.

ANATOMICAL GUIDE: MALE PROBOSCIS MONKEYS

Proboscis monkeys are known in Malay as *Monyet Belanda* (Dutch Monkeys). It is estimated that fewer than 8,000 of them remain in the wild in Borneo.

Arms
The monkeys throw themselves into a freefall and then catch themselves as they land. When outstretched, the arms aid them in sailing from tree to tree.

Potbelly
Large stomach with a complex, bacteria-filled digestive system aids in digesting seeds, leaves and unripened fruits (sweet fruits are typically avoided as they can lead to rapid fermentation, and eventually, to death by bloating). Altogether the stomach and its contents constitute about a quarter of the animal's weight.

Nose
Oversized, pendulous nose Seen only in males, the size of the nose is believed to be crucial in attracting females; their noses sometimes get so large that they have to be lifted out of the way in order for food to be put into the mouth. The nose is also instrumental in creating honking sounds, the larger the nose, the deeper and more resonant the honk.

Penis
The penis is almost permanently erect and bright red.

Tail
The tail aids in balance, but is not used for gripping.

CINEMA ADMISSIONS BY FILM LANGUAGE (MILLION PERSONS)

Year	Malay	Chinese	Tamil	English	Indonesian	Others	Total
2017	4.52	6.81	4.82	54.19	0.94	1.56	**72.84**
2018	13.21	5.34	4.45	51.76	0.82	1.73	**77.31**
2019	11.61	6.67	4.82	52.02	1.10	1.56	**77.78**
2020	2.98	1.77	0.73	4.40	0.12	0.96	**10.96**
2021	0.82	0.20	0.145	0.93	0.645	0.00	**2.36**
2022	0.29	0.24	0.145	0.93	0.645	0.11	**2.36**

Source: National Film Development Corporation Malaysia (FINAS)

CASES TRIED BEFORE THE REGISTRAR AGAINST RICKSHAW DRIVERS

Offence	1895	1905	1915
Bad clothes	3,795	15	–
Behaving rudely	28	175	192
Endangering traffic	441	255	1,094
Employing unfit coolies	102	221	255
Loitering and obstruction	12,355	2,594	1,395
Refusing hire	474	152	–
Refusing fare	230	50	–
Soliciting in a disorderly manner	2,393	856	1,376
Other	1,503	1,568	1,690
Total	**21,321**	**5,886**	**6,002**
Convicted	19,778	5,002	5,000

Source: *The Underside of Malaysian History* by Peter Rimmer and Lisa Allen, 1990

YAM SENG!

"*Yam seng*" is Cantonese for "cheers". A tin mine in Malaysia came to be called by this name. The Irish owner of the tin mine went back to his home city of Dublin to register the mine. He had all his papers with him. The solicitor read these through and when he found everything in order, he drew up the final document and all that had to be added was the intended name of the mine.

He asked the owner, "Well, what are you going to call it?"

The owner cogitated and picked up his glass containing John Jamieson 12 Year Old Irish Whiskey and lifting his glass, said "*yam seng*!"

The solicitor duly filled this in as the name of the mine. When the owner realised what had happened, he laughed and said, "Well, that is a very appropriate name for a tin mine, "bottoms up", I think we will just leave it at that."

Henceforth, it was called the Yam Seng Mine, owned by the Yam Seng Mining Company.

Source: *Tales from Raffles* by Charles B. Wilson, 1968

THE HIGHEST AWARD FOR ARTISTS AND WRITERS

Anugerah Seni Negara (National Art Award)

Winners receive:

RM60,000, a trophy, a *songket baju melayu* set, and free medical treatment at the first class ward of any government hospital.

Recipients:

1993	Hamzah Awang Hamat (*wayang kulit* puppeteer)
1995	Datuk Syed Ahmad Jamal (artist)
1997	Haji Wan Su Othman (carver)
1999	Khadijah Awang (*Mak Yong* expert)
2002	Datuk Syed Alwi Syed Hassan (playwright)
2004	Rahman B (*Bangsawan* performer)
2006	Datuk Ahmad Nawab (composer)
2008	Tan Sri Jins Shamsuddin (actor, film director, film producer)

Anugerah Sastera Negara (National Literary Award)

Winners receive:

RM60,000, scroll of national recognition, writing and publishing facilities, free medical treatment at the first class ward of any government hospital.

Recipients:

1981	Kamaludin Muhammad (pen name: Keris Mas)
1982	Datuk Haji Shahnon Ahmad
1983	Datuk Dr Usman Awang
1985	Datuk Dr A. Samad Said
1987	Muhammad bin Abdul Biang (pen name: Arena Wati)
1991	Prof. Dr Muhammad Haji Salleh
1993	Datuk Noordin Hassan
1996	Datuk Haji Abdullah bin Hussain
2003	Syed Othman Syed Omar (pen name: S. Othman Kelantan)
2009	Datuk Dr Mohd Anuar Rethwan (Anwar Ridhwan)
2011	Datuk Dr. Ahmad Kamal Abdullah atau Kemala
2013	Datuk Baha Zain
2015	Datuk Dr. Zurinah Hassan
2019	Prof. Dr. Siti Zainon Ismail
2022	Dato' Rahman Shaari

EARTH GOD OF THE MALAYSIAN CHINESE

Na Tuk Kong is a local earth deity whose name is derived from the combination of the Malay word "*datuk*" with the Cantonese word "*kong*", both of which are honorific titles used to address elders. Na Tuk Kong is usually represented as an old holy man, and shrines devoted to him can be found outside houses and on the roadsides in Chinese communities. Common offerings to Na Tuk Kong include candles, joss sticks, burning gum as well as shredded tobacco, areca nut flakes, betel leaves with lime paste and fruits.

BELIEVE IT OR NOT: MALACCA LEGENDS

On his way to Malacca in 1546, Francis Xavier (later Saint Francis Xavier) got caught in a terrible storm and his boat nearly capsized. In a gesture of faith, he held his crucifix in his hand and said a prayer, asking god to calm the turbulent waters, and then proceeded to throw his cross into the sea. The storm then ceased and the sea calmed down. But, unfortunately, Saint Francis had lost his crucifix. However, when he landed on the shores of Malacca, he saw a crab crawling towards him, holding the crucifix in its claws. He picked up the cross and blessed the crab. To this day, a species of crab that bears the sign of the cross on its shell can be found in the Strait of Malacca.

· · ·

In the 1460s, during the reign of the second sultan of Malacca, Mansur Shah, a Chinese ship arrived in the Malacca port filled with valuable gold needles and a message from the Emperor of China: "For every gold needle I have a subject, if you could count their number, then you would know my power." The sultan sent back a ship stuffed with bags of sago and containing the message: "If you can count the grains of sago on this ship you will have guessed the number of my subjects correctly, and you will know my power." The Chinese emperor, deeply impressed, then sent his daughter, Hang Li Poh, to marry the sultan.

THE FIRST "MALAYSIAN" COMPUTERS

On 1 August 2008, the Malaysian Institute of Microelectronic Systems (MIMOS) Berhad unveiled the first range of computers developed in Malaysia, named "Mak Cik" (old aunt). The first two models were named the "i-Dola" laptop and "Jean-i" personal computer (PC) after the Prime Minister and his wife respectively. The computers, debuting at RM1,000 (laptop) and RM500 (PC), were to be manufactured in Zambia.
Source: *The Star*

ANCIENT REMAINS

Some artefacts excavated from 4th- to 11th-century Buddhist temples in the Bujang Valley in Kedah:

- Closed reliquaries with chambers containing jars of beads
- Gold and silver foil in the shape of a Nandi bull and female divinity holding a lotus flower and a trident
- A bronze statue pedestal
- A bronze trident belonging to the god Siva
- A bronze reliquary containing gemstones
- A gold bowl, rings, and earrings
- A golden lion, silver bull and copper horse
- Bells and lamps
- A finger and an aureole from a statuette
- Terracotta Buddha, elephant and Boddhisattva statuettes
- A bronze statuette representing the goddess Bhrkuti
- Bricks inscribed with Pallava letters and marked with animal footprints
- Ceramic shards
- Iron nails
- Beads of various colours and shapes

The artefacts, along with many others, are now housed in the Lembah Bujang Archaeological Museum in Merbok, Kedah.

ELEPHANT HUNTING IN 19TH-CENTURY BORNEO

"No elephant has yet been bagged by a European. Frank Hatton had shot at and wounded one on the occasion when he met with his fatal accident, and one or two others have been shot at from time to time. Europeans, when they go into the forest, are usually on business—exploring, path-cutting, surveying, and the like—and the noise made by the number of coolies and carriers that accompany them frightens all game away... The natives occasionally shoot elephants, and one or two of their tusks are generally on sale in the Bazaar. They usually fetch a rather higher price, and are sent over to Sooloo to be converted into creese handles. The proportion of tuskers may be taken to be about one in four; of four elephants that some Booloodoopies* shot at Terruttum (in Dewhurst Bay), one only was a tusker..."

—From *The Handbook of British North Borneo*, 1890.
* British term for one of the tribes of native Borneans.

GENDER IN THE MARKETPLACE

The ground floor of the main market, the Siti Khadijah market, in Kota Bharu, Kelantan, is divided into male- and female-vendor territories.

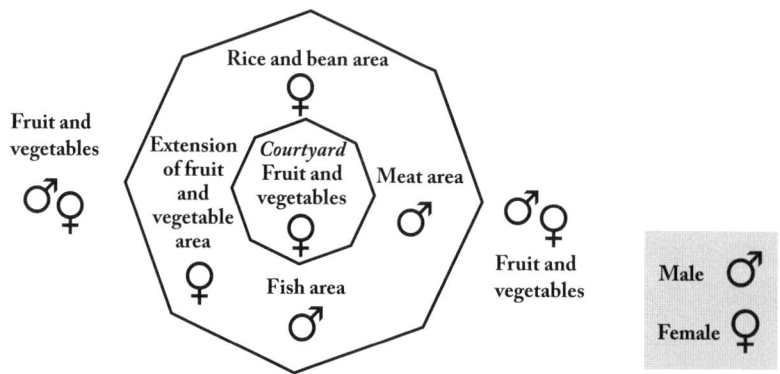

Source: *Visible Women in East Coast Malay Society* by Ingrid Rudie, 1994

EXTREME WEATHER

40.1°C	Highest temperature	Chuping, Perlis on 9 April 1998
7.8°C	Lowest temperature	Cameron Highlands, Pahang on 1 February 1978
1.1°C	Lowest temperature variation in one day	Cameron Highlands, Pahang on 16 November 1998
15.7°C	Greatest temperature variation in one day	Kuala Krai, Kelantan on 20 April 1998
159.4 mm	Highest rainfall in an hour	Sandakan, Sabah on 27 October 2006
608 mm	Highest rainfall in a day	Kota Bharu, Kelantan on 6 January 1967
5,687 mm	Highest rainfall in a year	Sandakan, Sabah in 2006
1,151 mm	Lowest rainfall in a year	Tawau, Sabah in 1997
41.7 m/s	Highest maximum wind speed	Kuching, Sarawak on 15 September 1992
362 days	Highest number of days with lightning in a year	Subang, Selangor in 1987

Source: Malaysian Meteorological Department

SOME MALAYSIAN WORLD RECORD ACHIEVERS

Plane pulling
Using his hair, R. Letchemanah dragged a 32.5-tonne Boeing 737 over a distance of 16.85 metres at the Sultan Abdul Aziz Shah Airport in Subang in 1990.

Tallest pencil
The 20.248-metre pencil, housed at the Faber-Castell's premises in Subang Jaya, is the world's tallest. It is made of kiln-dried Jelutong sawn timber.

Largest bean art
It took two days and two hours for 500 students and volunteers from the Central Academy of Art in Kuala Lumpur to complete a 31.7-metre-long and 26.8-metre- wide "Buddhism Auspicious" design made from 12 tonnes of beans.

Largest pewter tankard
In commemoration of its centenary, Royal Selangor Pewter crafted the world's biggest pewter tankard, which stands at 1.987 metres in height and has a volume capacity of 2,796 litres.

Longest coin line
Over 500 volunteers created a 55.63-kilometre line of 20-sen coins at Dataran Merdeka in 1995.

First arm transplant
In 2000, four-week-old Chong Lih Ying became the first and youngest person in the world to undergo a whole-limb transplant when she had an arm attached to her deformed limb at the Selayang Hospital in Selangor.

Most eggs crushed with a wrist
In 2005, Sivasamy Balakrishnan crushed 25 eggs in 30 seconds at his workplace, the Naina Mohammed restaurant in Ipoh. He placed the eggs on the back of his wrist and bent his fingers backwards to break them.

Longest abbreviation
The world's longest known abbreviation is S.K.O.M.K.H.P.K.J.C.D.P.W.B. which stands for Syarikat Kerjasama Orang-Orang Melayu Kerajaan Hilir Perak Kerana Jimat Cermat Dan Pinjam-Meninjam Wang Berhad.

Most frequent best man
Ting Ming Siong of Sarawak has served as a best man at weddings 1,395 times since 1975.

Source: *Malaysian Book of Records*, 2007

SAY WHAT?

The national flag is a banner Gules, seven bars Argent; the canton Azure is charged with decrescent and mullet of fourteen points.

This means it is a red flag with seven horizontal white stripes; the upper-left (hoist) quarter is blue with a yellow waning crescent and a yellow 14-pointed star.

HOW TO ADDRESS MALAYSIAN ROYALTY

Title	English equivalent	Honorific
Yang di-Pertuan Agong	Paramount Ruler	Seri Paduka Baginda
Raja Permaisuri Agong	Queen	Seri Paduka Baginda
Sultan, Raja, Yang di-Pertuan Besar	Royal Head-of-State	Duli Yang Maha Mulia
Sultanah, Raja Perempuan, Tengku Ampuan, Raja Permaisuri, Tengku Permaisuri	Official consort of a Royal Head of State	Duli Yang Maha Mulia

Source: Adapted from *Malaysian Customs and Etiquette* by Dato' Paduka Noor Aini Abdullah-Amir, 2000

CODES OF AIRPORTS IN PENINSULAR MALAYSIA

- AOR (Alor Star)
- BWH (Butterworth)
- JHB (Senai International Airport, near Johor Bahru)
- KTE (Kerteh, Terengganu)
- KUA (Kuantan)
- KUL (Kuala Lumpur International Airport)
- LGK (Langkawi International Airport)
- MEP (Mersing)
- MKZ (Malacca International Airport)
- PEN (Penang International Airport)
- PKG (Pangkor)
- RDN (Redang)
- SWY (Sitiawan Airport)
- SZB (Sultan Abdul Aziz Shah Airport / RMAF Subang)
- TGG (Kuala Terengganu)
- TOD (Tioman)
- TPG (Taiping)
- WMAP (Kluang)
- WMGK (Gong Kedak)
- WMKF (Sungai Besi)

SOME OF THE SHAPES OF MALAYSIA

National Mosque,
Kuala Lumpur

Sepang International
Circuit

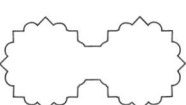

Petronas Twin Towers,
Kuala Lumpur

Menara TM,
Kuala Lumpur

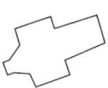

Christchurch, Malacca

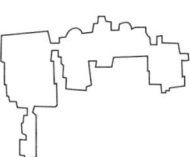

Istana Negara,
Kuala Lumpur

VIEWER DISCRETION ADVISED

Films approved for public viewing by the Film Censorship Board are classified as follows:

- **U** (Umum or "general audiences"): For general audiences.
- **P13**: Parental guidance suggested for children under the age of 13.
- **18SG** (Seram, Ganas or "violence" and "horror"): Viewers under the age of 18 are prohibited due to the fact that the film may contain elements of violence or horror that they may find objectionable.
- **18SX** (Seks or "sex"): Viewers under the age of 18 are prohibited due to the fact that the film may contain sex scenes, nudity or sexual dialogues or references that they may find objectionable.
- **18PA** (Politik, Agama or "politics" and "religion"): Viewers under the age of 18 are prohibited due to the fact that the film may contain religious, social or political aspects that they may find objectionable.
- **18PL** (Pelbagai, or "variety"): Viewers under 18 are prohibited due to the fact that the film may contain strong violence, gore, horror or terror, sex scenes, nudity, sexual dialogues or references, or religious, social or political aspects they may find objectionable.

The number of landslide incidents reported in Malaysia during the monsoon 2021-22:

THE ROYAL SELANGOR CLUB

Founded in 1884, the Royal Selangor Club was nicknamed "The Spotted Dog" because two Dalmatians belonging to the wife of one of the club founders were left to guard the entrance whenever they visited the club. The club is also referred to as "The Gay Old Dog" or "The Dog".

"Ladies and children below 18 years are not allowed"
— So states a sign outside the Long Bar at the Royal Selangor Club. Women are purportedly banned because men "drink and get very excited when they watch the games and they didn't want the ladies to see their exuberant behaviour".

FROM POP HIT TO REGAL ANTHEM

The national anthem, *Negaraku*, was adapted from the state anthem of Perak. But before it was a ceremonial accompaniment to regal occasions in Perak, the song—with lyrics added to a tune composed by Frenchman Pierre-Jean de Beranger (1780–1857)—was a popular number in the Seychelles.

The sultan of Perak, Sultan Abdullah—living in exile in the Seychelles in the late 1800s—was captivated by the song.

The tune became a pop hit, entitled *Terang Bulan*, when an Indonesian *bangsawan* troupe introduced it in performances in Singapore in the early twentieth century.

At a reception in Europe c. 1900, when an aide of the then sultan of Perak, Sultan Idris, was asked about the anthem for his state and not wanting to reveal a lack of one, he hummed the tune.

When Malaya attained independence in 1957, a worldwide competition was held to select a national anthem. Five hundred and fourteen compositions were submitted, but none struck the right notes to the vetting committee. Invitations were then extended to Benjamin Britten, Sir William Walton (who had just composed the march for Queen Elizabeth II's coronation), Gian Carlo Menotti and Zubir Said (who later composed the national anthem for Singapore). Again, the compositions that were submitted didn't ring true.

Hence, the eventual settling on the state anthem of Perak, with re-written lyrics.

Source: Perpustakaan Negara Malaysia

SOME OF THE ARCHITECTS OF MALAYSIA

Ahmad Rozi Abdul Wahab	Perdana Putra (1999)
Howard Ashley, Ikmal Hisham Albakri and Baharuddin Kassim	National Mosque (1965)
Regent Alfred John Bidwell	Sultan Abdul Samad Building (1897)
Hijjas Kasturi	Tabung Haji (1984), Menara Maybank (1988), Tun Sambanthan Building (1988), Shah Alam Stadium (1994), Citibank Building (1995), Telekom Malaysia Headquarters (2001), Sarawak Parliament Building (2009)
Ikmal Hisham Albakri and Victor Chew	Putra World Trade Centre (1984), National Library (1994)
Arthur Bennison Hubback	Jamek Mosque (1909), Kuala Lumpur Railway Station (1911), Ipoh Railway Station (1917), Ubudiah Mosque (1917)
S.E. Jewkes	Stadium Negara (1962)
T.Y. Lee	Central Market (1936), Chin Woo Stadium (1953), UMNO Building, Kuala Lumpur (1955), Dewan Bahasa Dan Pustaka (1956)
Arthur Charles Alfred Norman	Court of Justice (1880s), Selangor Club (1890), St. Mary's Church (1894), Victoria Institution (1894), Pudu Jail (1895), old Kuala Lumpur General Post Office (1896), Carcosa (1897)
César Pelli	Petronas Twin Towers (1998)
Kevin Roche, John Dinkeloo and Associates	Maxis Tower (1998)
William Ivor Shipley	Parliament House (1963)
Ho Kwong Yew & Sons	Muzium Negara (1963)
Ken Yeang	Mesiniaga Building, Subang Jaya (1992), UMNO Tower, Penang (1998), Mesiniaga Building, Penang (2003)
Peter Chan	The Exchange 106 (2019)
Fender Katsalidis	Merdeka 118 (2022)

Age in years of the oldest rubber tree in Malaysia, planted by Sir Hugh Low in Kuala Kangsar:

MYKAD NUMBER: WHAT IT MEANS

MyKad, or Government Multipurpose Card (GMPC), is the official compulsory identity card of Malaysia. It is regarded as the world's first smart identity card.

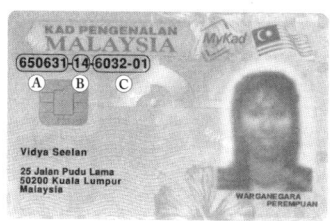 

A. Date of birth (YYMMDD)
B. Place of birth (state) code.
C. Generic serial number. If it ends with an odd number, it denotes the cardholder is male, while an even number denotes a female cardholder.
D. Stated only on the back of the MyKad. Denotes the number of identity cards the owner previously held.
E. The cardholder's old identity card number.

SOME FERMENTED MALAYSIAN FOODS

Local name	Fermented...
Belacan	shrimp paste
Budu	anchovies
Cencaluk	shrimps
Chau tau fu	tofu
Fu yue	beancurd
Ha kow	shrimp paste
Ikan pekasam	fish
Tairu/Morru	milk (essentially yoghurt)
Tapai pulut	glutinous rice
Tapai ubi	Cassava (tapioca) tubers
Tau chu	soy
Tau si	black beans
Tempoyak	durian

RECENTLY REPORTED TIGER ENCOUNTERS

Date	Location	Casualty	Details of attack
5.3.2001	Jeli, Kelantan	Abdullah Hamat and Siti Hawa Daud, rubber tappers	Attacked on their way to work. Nearly killed.
3.4.2001	Kuala Krai, Kelantan	Villagers of Stong	Tiger ran amok in the village. Nobody was injured.
25.5.2001	Hulu Terengganu, Terengganu	Mohd Fausi Ismail, farmer	Attacked at his family's Terengganu pineapple plantation.
9.7.2001	Jeli, Kelantan	Mohd Zaid Abdul Manaf, rubber tapper	Mauled to death.
18.3.2002	Kuala Krai, Kelantan	Rubber plantation workers	A tiger chased 12 plantation workers. Nobody was hurt.
21.4.2002	Tanah Merah, Kelantan	Mohamad Nor Abdul Rahman, rubber tapper	Mauled to death.
5.5.2002	Jeli, Kelantan	Nik Mariam Ibrahim, rubber tapper	Mauled to death.
23.5.2002	Pekan, Pahang	Linggi, Orang Asli	Severely injured on his left leg, and had to have it amputated. Attacked on his way back from foraging for agar wood (gaharu).
9.7.2002	Jeli, Kelantan	Siti Eshah Mamat, rubber tapper	Mauled to death.
4.8.2002	Jeli, Kelantan	Abdullah Hamat, rubber tapper	Sustained serious facial injuries and received 200 stitches.
24.8.2002	Gua Musang, Kelantan	Baauk An Hang, Orang Asli	Attacked while hunting for monkeys with his brother. Seriously injured and sustained a broken jaw.
26.8.2005	Jeli, Kelantan	Rokiah Latif, rubber tapper	Mauled to death.
26.11.2007	Jeli, Kelantan	Mek Jah Ismail, rubber tapper	Sustained serious injuries.
19.5.2022	Ampang	–	Police receive a report (later found to be untrue) of a tiger standing near a lamp post in Ulu Kelang.
9.7.2022	Not stated	–	Conservationists from World Wildlife Fund-Malaysia reveal that they spotted a tigress and her four cubs earlier that year.

Note: No tiger attacks were reported in 2006, and none have been reported since 2007.
Source: Department of Wildlife and National Parks

CHANGING NAMES OF FAMOUS STREETS

The majority of roads in big towns and cities in Malaysia built during the British administration in the country bore English names, including those of British administrators. After Independence in 1957 and the formation of Malaysia in 1963, many of these street names were translated into the Malay language. Although some names of British administrators have been retained, many have been renamed after prominent Malaysians.

The following are some streets in Kuala Lumpur that have been renamed:

Current name	Former name
Jalan Sultan Salahuddin (The 11th Yang di-Pertuan Agong of Malaysia and eighth sultan of Selangor)	**Swettenham Road** (Sir Frank Swettenham, resident-general from 1896 to 1901)
Jalan Hang Jebat (A warrior of Malacca)	**Davidson Road** (James Guthrie Davidson, Resident of Selangor, 1875-76, then Resident in Perak, 1876-77)
Jalan Dato' Onn (Dato' Onn Jaafar was founder of the United Malays National Organisation (UMNO))	**Brockman Road** (Sir Edward Lewis Brockman, chief secretary to the Federated Malay States (FMS) from 1911 to 1920, resident of Pahang from 1909 to 1910)
Jalan Raja Chulan (A member of the Perak royal family)	**Weld Road** (Sir Frederick Weld, governor of the Straits Settlements from 1880 to 1887)
Jalan Sultan Ismail (Third sultan of Johor)	**Treacher Road** (Sir William Hood Treacher, resident-general of the FMS from 1901 to 1904)
Jalan Tun Perak (Bendahara or prime minister of the Malacca Sultanate during the 15th century)	**Mountbatten Road** (Lord Louis Mountbatten, allied supreme commander in Southeast Asia during World War II. Formerly named Java Street)
Jalan Hang Tuah (A famous warrior of the Malacca Sultanate)	**Shaw Road** (Bennett E. Shaw, first principal of Victoria Institution and renowned educationist in Malaya. Formerly named Gaol Road after the Pudu Jail)
Jalan Maharajalela (Malay chieftain who was instrumental in the assassination of J.W.W. Birch)	**Birch Road** (J.W.W. Birch, the first resident of Perak from 1874 to 1875; he was assassinated)
Jalan Tun Razak (Second prime minister of Malaysia)	**Circular Road** (Changed to Jalan Pekeliling, a translation of Circular Road, before assuming the current name)

SOME ORANG-UTAN SOUNDS AND THEIR MEANINGS

Sound	Description	Situation
Frustrated scream	Long, wavering screams	Young animals when food withheld
Kiss squeak	Sharp intake of air through trumpet lips	Excitement or fear
Raspberry	Sharp expulsion of air through trumpet lips	Excitement or fear
Soft hoots	Pout-faced hoots	Young animals when worried
Long calls	Very loud series of groans	For males to let females know their whereabouts
Mating cries	Loud piercing shrieks	Females during mating
Rape cries	Deep grunts	Female during rape
Play grunts	Huffy "haah" noises	During intensive play
'Grumphs'	Deep throaty grumps and gulps	Warning display

Source: *Orang-Utans in Borneo* by Gisela Kaplan and Lesley Rogers, 1994

THE SHOW MUST GO ON AT ISTANA BUDAYA

Production	Year	Number of performances	Total audience	Average attendance per show
Cats: The Musical	2002	37	**32,160**	869
Mamma Mia!	2008	24	**30,000**	1,250
Puteri Gunung Ledang (Season 1)	2006	23	**27,672**	1,203
Puteri Gunung Ledang (Season 2)	2006	18	**23,015**	1,278
The Sound of Music	2005	23	**22,745**	989
P. Ramlee: The Musical (Season 1)	2007	17	**21,830**	1,284
P. Ramlee: The Musical (Season 2)	2008	20	**20,954**	1,048
P. Ramlee: The Musical	2014	15	**16,225**	1,082
Fame: The Musical	2002	23	**19,348**	841
Saturday Night Fever	2004	24	**18,745**	781
Stomp	2005	13	**15,920**	1,224

Source: Istana Budaya

Average height in centimetres of adult female orang-utans:

WARNING TO DRUG TRAFFICKERS

In Malaysia, the Dangerous Drugs Act 1952, under Section 39B, provides for a mandatory death sentence for anyone found guilty of possessing and distributing illegal drugs. Any person who is found in possession of the amount of the drugs listed below otherwise than in accordance with the authority of this Act or any written law, will be presumed, until the contrary is proved, to be trafficking in the said drug.

Drug	Minimum weight in grams
Amphetamine or Methamphetamine	50
Cannabis or cannabis resin	200
Cocaine	40
Heroin or morphine	15
Prepared and/or raw opium	1000

Note: Since 1980, over 270 people have been hanged in Malaysia, mostly for drug-related crimes.

HOW A FAMOSA WAS DESTROYED

The following excerpt from the *Hikayat Abdullah* relates an eyewitness account of the destruction of A Famosa (a Portuguese fort built in Malacca in 1511) by the British in 1806.

"Mr. Farquhar, the Resident, set about demolishing the Malacca fort. He called coolies of all races together and bid them smash the fort first from the Bukit China side. Hundreds of coolies tried to break the stone, but after two or three days they were unable to do so for they were afraid because they fully believed there were ghosts and devils in the fort.

When Mr. Farquhar saw how difficult it was to smash the stone he gave instructions to dig down to the foundations of the fort. But however deep the coolies dug, the foundations of the fort were not reached.

After about three months of illness and trouble, with many men dying or breaking their arms and legs, news was suddenly heard that the Resident was ordering a hole to be dug under the bastion on the seaward side of the fort, in which boxes of gunpowder were to be placed for firing. Then orders were given to close the hole, and stones and earth were rammed down tight inside.

A gong was sounded, and it was announced that the next day at eight o'clock no one was to cross the river, and those living in houses close by were told to move to others far away. The next morning Mr. Farquhar appeared on horseback holding a slow match in his hand. He touched off the fuse and at once spurred his horse away. After about ten minutes the gunpowder exploded with a noise like thunder, and pieces of the fort as large as elephants, and some as large as houses, were blown into the air and cascaded into the sea.

Now by the will of Allah, the fort was no more, showing how ephemeral are the things of this world. The old order was destroyed, a new world was created and all around us was changed."

LICENCE PLATES

The Jabatan Pengangkutan Jalan Malaysia (JPJ, or Malaysian Road Transport Department) allows for three forms of vehicle registration number plates:

1. White letters and numerals fixed or embossed on a black frame.
2. White letters and numerals fixed or embossed on a red frame for vehicles belonging to embassies, United Nations and the International Natural Rubber Association.
3. Black letters and numerals fixed or embossed on a white frame for taxis or hired cars.

Most recently issued licence plate numbers by state or district as at 3 August 2009.

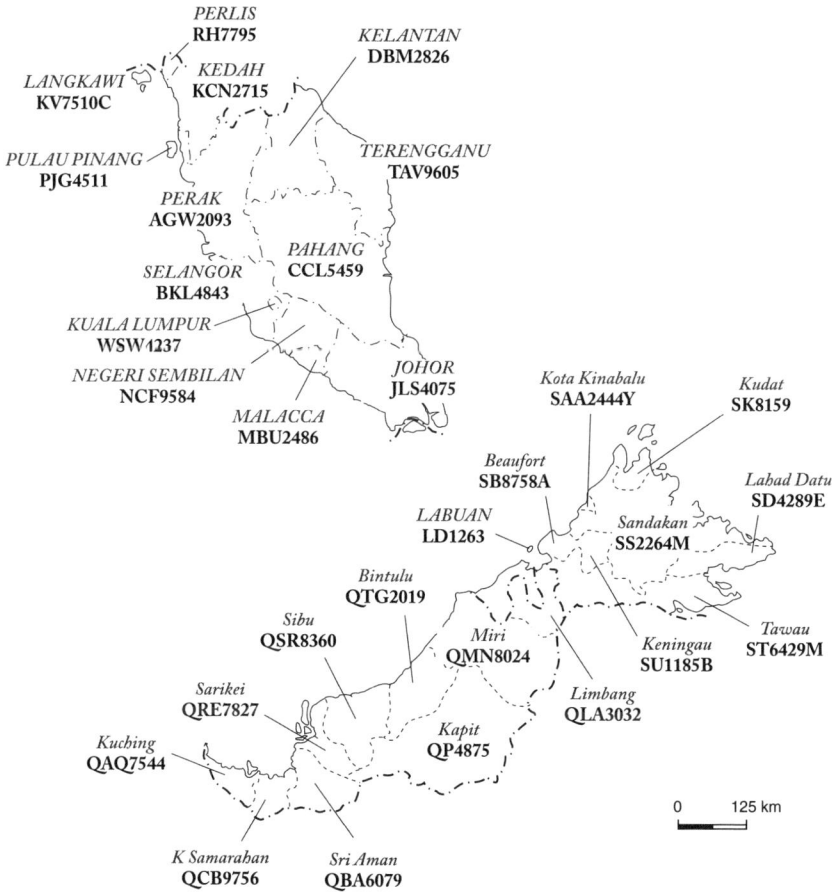

PERLIS RH7795
KELANTAN DBM2826
LANGKAWI KV7510C
KEDAH KCN2715
PULAU PINANG PJG4511
TERENGGANU TAV9605
PERAK AGW2093
PAHANG CCL5459
SELANGOR BKL4843
KUALA LUMPUR WSW4237
NEGERI SEMBILAN NCF9584
JOHOR JLS4075
MALACCA MBU2486
Kota Kinabalu SAA2444Y
Kudat SK8159
Beaufort SB8758A
Labad Datu SD4289E
LABUAN LD1263
Sandakan SS2264M
Bintulu QTG2019
Sibu QSR8360
Miri QMN8024
Keningau SU1185B
Tawau ST6429M
Sarikei QRE7832
Limbang QLA3032
Kuching QAQ7544
Kapit QP4875
K Samarahan QCB9756
Sri Aman QBA6079

A VERY ROUGH GUIDE

A translation of a 15th-century Arab's description of the sailing routes around the southern part of the Malay Peninsula. The directions were couched in poetic metre so that they might more easily be committed to memory.

>And if you...would leave the islands of Pulau Sanbilan
>Navigate by the rising of the Scorpion's heart to Qafasi
>And you will come to grief.
>For, from Dang-Dang and Pulau Sanbilan, deviate not.
>As for the route to Johor, this fortress, and to Pulau Berhala...
>Set course by the Crown rejoicing the Berhala also with Johor;
>And if you would leave these behind, set the compass on the small Dog-Star and be not slow
>To Mal'aqa. Listen to my positions, and the water will be 10 fathoms.
>He will come before Mal'aqa, and perceive Fal Fasalar with al-Qafasi, and know
>Fal Fasalar is a mountain, and Qafasi is an abundance of shallows in the water,
>Where are gaps, O my brother, when you see Fal Fasalar with Simak, then give thanks,
>And if you desire the land of Mal'aqa, then rely upon the small star of the Dog,
>Till near Singapur, then travel thence towards Taik by the Great Bear
>Then steer from Tinggi in the direction of Sura by the setting of the famous seven.

INTERNAL SECURITY ACT DETAINEES SINCE 2004-2009

Reason detained	Number of detainees
Forging of documents	29
Involvement in Jemaah Islamiah	18
Duplication of RM1 coins	17
Involvement in Darul Islam	17
Acting as foreign intelligence agents	7
Involvement in Hindraf	5
Involvement in Thai Separatist Movement	3
Involvement in Malaysia Militant Group	1
Producing writings insulting Islam	1
Smuggling illegal immigrants	1
Nuclear component supplier	1
Total	**100**

Source: *The Sun*, 26 June 2009

A SELECTION OF THE LONGEST

Longest **river**	Sungai Rajang, Sarawak (563 km)
Longest **underground tunnel**	Sungai Lembing mine, Pahang (322 km)
Longest **bridge**	Second Penang Bridge (24 km)
Longest **river bridge**	Sungai Dinding Bridge, Pahang (1.25 km)
Longest **tunnel**	Stormwater Management and Road Tunnel (SMART), Kuala Lumpur (9.7 km)
Longest **canopy walkway**	Sungai Sedim Recreational Park (925 m)
Longest **pedestrian suspension bridge**	Langkawi Sky Bridge (125 m)
Longest **underwater limestone cave**	Kaki Bukit, Perlis (370 m)
Longest **dragon statue**	Fortune Dragon or Prosperity Dragon, Batu Pahat (115 m)
Longest **train tunnel**	Bukit Berapit Rail Tunnel (3.3 km)
Longest **sand sculpture**	Cheras, Kuala Lumpur (210 m)
Longest **roofing sheet**	Proton plant, Shah Alam (131 m)
Longest **snake**	Port Dickson, Negeri Sembilan (5.5 m)

HOW TO START A SUCCESSFUL SWIFTLET FARM

1. Identify and rent or, preferably, purchase a building that has the potential to be converted into a successful swiftlet farm. The building must be located where there are signs of swiftlet activity and it must not be obstructed by other buildings.

2. Remove the top floor ceiling and put meranti wood plank frames and ceiling boards in place.

3. Mount steel plates on top of the ceiling boards in order to enhance roof stability and security.

4. Erect brick walls on the inside of the front and back windows of the building to prevent break-ins. Make sure that each wall is equipped with numerous ventilation points. Cover the walls with cement.

5. Buy a CD player, install internal and external speakers in your building and broadcast chirping sounds to encourage the swiftlets to visit and reside in your farm.

6. Install a humidifier system to maintain the farm's humidity at around 75–80 per cent.

7. Wait for the swiftlets to come and build their nests. Do not harvest the nests with eggs or hatchlings inside.

Source: *Make Millions from Swiftlet Farming: A Definitive Guide* by Dr Christopher Lim, 2007

ORIGINS OF SOME MALAY WORDS

Borrowed from	Malay word	Original word	Meaning
Portuguese	Almari	Armário	Cupboard
	Bendera	Bandeira	Flag
	Garfu	Garfo	Fork
	Gereja	Igreja	Church
	Limau	Limão	Lemon
	Bomba	Bomba	Fire brigade
	Kereta	Carreta	Car
Tamil	Kapal	Kappal	Ship
	Katil	Kattil	Bed
	Kuda	Kudh	Horse
	Satay	Sathai	Flesh
Persian	Anggur	Angur	Grape
	Bandar	Bandr	Town
	Dewan	Diwan	Hall
	Gandum	Gandm	Wheat
	Kurma	khurma	Date (fruit)
Sanskrit	Bahasa	Bhāshā	Language
	Buat	Wuat	To do
	Bumi	Bhumi	Earth
	Kepala	Kapala	Skull or head
	Manusia	Manusya	Human being
Hokkien (Chinese dialect)	Bihun	Bi-hun	Rice vermicelli
	Mi	Mee	Noodles
	Kongsi	Kong-si	To share
Dutch	Aksi	Actie	Action
	Buku	Boek	Book
Arabic	Dunia	Dunyā	World
	Makhluk	Makluq	Creatures
	Ilmu	ilm	Knowledge
	Sultan	Sultan	Sultan

WE COULD HAVE BEEN LANGKASUKANS

When Malaya was planning to join together with Sabah and Sarawak in 1963, one of the names considered for the new political entity was Langkasuka. Langkasuka was an ancient (probably the earliest) Hindu–Buddhist–Khmer–Malay kingdom that was founded in the first or second century CE in the north of the country. Its name was probably a derivation of two Sanskrit words, *langkha* meaning "resplendent land" and *sikkha* meaning "bliss".

Records from the Liang Dynasty of China (500 CE) refer to the kingdom of *Lang-ya-xin* founded in the 1st century CE. Its span was a 30-day journey east-to-west and a 20-day trek north-to-south. The capital was described as surrounded by walls with double gates and towers, and pavilions. The inhabitants were largely Khmers ruled by Hindu kings.

Over a millennium and a half, the kingdom's name in Chinese records kept changing—*Lang-ya-se-chia* during the Song Dynasty (960-1279); *Long-ya-si-jiao* during the Yuan Dynasty (1279-1368); *Lang-se-chia* during the Ming (1368-1644). At some point, it became a tributary of the Srivijaya Kingdom, and by the 15th century it was replaced by the Pattani Kingdom.

SILAT SCHOOL ADMISSION PROCEDURE

Before a pupil is formally accepted into a silat school, he must present his teacher with the following items:

- rice grains
- 2.5 yards of white cloth (a symbol of the purity and sincerity of the pupil's desire to learn the martial art. The cloth can also be used as a shroud in case of accidental death.)
- a knife
- some money
- seven needles (a symbol of the pupil's desire to practice consistently for the first seven days.)
- betel leaves and areca nuts

The instructor then recites a prayer and the pupil makes a pledge to use the knowledge of silat only for self-defence.

Source: *Silat Melayu* by Ku Ahmad bin Ku Mustaffa and Wong Kiew Kit, 1978

SELECTED SNAKEBITE MARKS

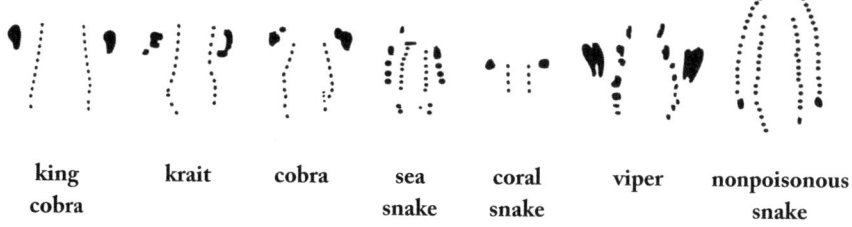

| king cobra | krait | cobra | sea snake | coral snake | viper | nonpoisonous snake |

PRICE OF ADMISSION

Political party	Registration fee	Annual membership	Lifetime membership
Democratic Action Party (DAP)	–	RM5	RM100
Malaysian Chinese Association (MCA)	–	RM2	RM100
Malaysian Indian Congress (MIC)	RM3	RM4	RM500
Parti Bersatu Sabah / Sabah United Party (PBS)	RM2	RM1	–
Parti Gerakan Rakyat Malaysia	RM2	RM2	based on selection
Parti Islam SeMalaysia (PAS)	RM2	RM3	RM100
Parti Keadilan Rakyat (PKR)	RM2	RM2	RM200
Sabah Progressive Party (SAPP)	RM2	RM1	not less than RM100
Sarawak United Peoples' Party (SUPP)	RM2	RM2	RM30
United Malays National Organisation (UMNO)	RM2	RM1	RM100
United Pasokmomogun Kadazandusun Murut Organisation (UPKO)	RM2	RM1	n/a

ITINERARY OF THE SPOOKSTER GHOST TOUR IN KUALA LUMPUR

- Meeting point
  Bangsar Seafood Village
  As many Asians believe that food helps to protect against the supernatural, the tour group will partake in a seafood dinner together. This is the last point on the tour at which you can back out.

- First stop
  Indian temple in Mid Valley City
  Mid Valley Megamall was built on the site of an Indian temple, which was subsequently renovated and rebuilt. Great care, however, was taken during the construction of the mall to preserve a particular tree that is believed to have been blessed by the gods.

- Second stop
  Seputeh Chinese cemetery
  Take a jaunt through this notorious 130-year-old Chinese cemetery (which is the burial place of Kuala Lumpur's founder, Yap Ah Loy) and feel the presence of the spirits that call this place home.

- Third stop
  Pudu Jail
  This now-defunct prison, which features a distinctive mural along its outer walls, was opened in 1891. As it has been the site of many deaths and executions over the years, it is believed to be haunted by countless ghosts and demons.

- Fourth stop
  Pontianak den
  Located in an exclusive area of Kuala Lumpur, the Pontianak den is the reputed domain of these beautiful female vampires, who are constantly on the prowl for fresh victims.

- Fifth stop
  Old Kuala Lumpur Railway Station
  Opened in 1910, this landmark was previously the scene of many suicides, as people used to jump off the road bridge in front of passing trains. As a result, many ghosts have been reported in the area.

- Ending point
  Bangsar Seafood Village
  You will undergo a final cleansing to ensure that no spirits follow you home.

Note: This two-hour tour is conducted nightly and costs RM168 per person.
Source: Asian Spooks Experience

The Eastern and Oriental Hotel in Penang is this number of years old:

SOME BASIC IBAN DESIGN MOTIFS

Lemiding fern curve	*Violin* head curve	*Hornbill* head curve	*Jempul* war knife hilt curve	*Kelindu* fern curve
Demam fern curve	*Wild betel* leaf curve	*Bear claw* curve	*Kubok* fern curve	*Prawn's* spear curve

LAND AREA AND POPULATION DENSITY

State	Area (km^2)	Percentage	Number of persons per km^2
Sarawak	124,450	37.62	20
Sabah	73,631	22.26	46
Pahang	36,137	10.92	44
Perak	21,035	6.36	118
Johor	19,210	5.81	209
Kelantan	15,099	4.56	119
Terengganu	13,035	3.94	89
Kedah	9,500	2.87	225
Selangor	8,104	2.45	880
Negeri Sembilan	6,686	2.02	180
Melaka	1,664	0.50	583
Penang	1,048	0.32	1659
Perlis	821	0.25	348
Kuala Lumpur (Federal Territory)	243	0.07	9,157
Labuan (Federal Territory)	91	0.03	1,034
Putrajaya (Federal Territory)	49	0.01	2,215
Total (Malaysia)	**330,803**	**100**	**98**

Source: Department of Statistics Malaysia, 2008 (area) and 2000 (density)

BODY LANGUAGE

The Malay language is descriptive, colourful and, at times, emphatic. In Malay idioms, the human body often symbolises one's character or abilities.

Idiom	Literal translation	Meaning
Otak (brain)		
Otak cermin	Mirror brain	Intelligent
Tajam otak	Sharp brain	Intelligent
Otak udang	A shrimp's brain	Stupid
Otak cair	Liquefied brain	Intelligent
Otak kering	Dry Brain	Slow on the uptake
Telinga (ears)		
Pasang telinga	To switch on one's ears	To listen carefully
Telinga kuali	Wok ears	One who is impervious to reprimand
Telinga lintah	Leech ears	One with good hearing
Telinga nipis	Thin ears	One who angers easily
Telinga tempayan	Waterjug-eared	One who refuses to listen
Mulut (mouth)		
Mulut murai	Mouth of a magpie	One who talks too much
Mulut tempayan	Waterjug-mouthed	Blabber mouth
Banyak mulut	Many mouths	One who talks too much
Berat mulut	Heavy-mouthed	One who does not say much
Pembasuh mulut	Mouth wash	Dessert
Perang mulut	War of the mouths	Heated debate or argument
Tangan (hand)		
Panjang tangan	Long arms	Compulsive thief
Campur tangan	Mixed hands	One who meddles or interferes

Hati (The Malay word hati refers to the liver. Idiomatically, however, hati refers to the heart or the state of the heart.)

Besar hati	Big heart	Elated, proud
Keras hati	Hard heart	Indomitable, stubborn
Susah hati	Difficult heart	Worried
Gelap hati	Dark heart	Sinister
Murah hati	Cheap heart	Generous
Lembut hati	Weak heart	Soft-hearted

The number of employees of the Royal Malaysia Police (in thousands):

BREEDS OF DOGS UNDER IMPORT CONTROL

Breeds of dogs banned from importation
- Pit Bull Terrier/Pit Bull (also known as American Pit Bull, American Pit Bull Terrier, American Staffordshire Terrier and Staffordshire Bull Terrier)
- American Bulldog
- Neapolitan Mastiff
- Japanese Tosa
- Akita
- Dogo Argentino
- Fila Braziliero

Restricted breeds of dogs (Importation subject to special conditions)
- Rottweiler
- Doberman
- German Shepherd/Alsatian, including Belgian Shepherd and East European Shepherd
- Bull Mastiff
- Bull Terrier
- Perro de Presa Canario (also known as Canary Dog)

Source: Department of Veterinary Services

NOTIFIABLE DISEASES (AMENDED 1998)

Under the Prevention and Control of Infectious Diseases Act 1988, every medical practitioner in Malaysia who treats or becomes aware of the existence of any infectious disease in any premises is required to report to the nearest Medical Officer of Health.

- **Immediate notification** (by phone, within 24 hours of diagnosis)
  Dengue fever and dengue haemorrhagic fever, yellow fever, diphtheria, ebola, food poisoning, plague, poliomyelitis (acute), rabies.

- **Notification within one week of diagnosis**
  Human Immunodeficiency Virus (HIV)/Acquired Immunodeficiency Syndrome (AIDS), whooping cough, measles, dysenteries, all forms of gonococcal infections, leprosy, malaria/myocarditis, relapsing fever, syphilis, tetanus, typhoid and paratyphoid fevers, typhus and other rickettsioses, all forms of tuberculosis, viral encephalitis, all forms of viral hepatitis, all forms of microbial infections.

FOOT REFLEXOLOGY

Chinese foot reflexology involves applying pressure to the patient's feet using the thumb, finger and hand as well as various tools and instruments. The underlying belief is that the body is reflected on the feet, which can be divided into different zones corresponding to various parts of the human anatomy. By applying pressure to these areas, the reflexologist can assess and improve the patient's health.

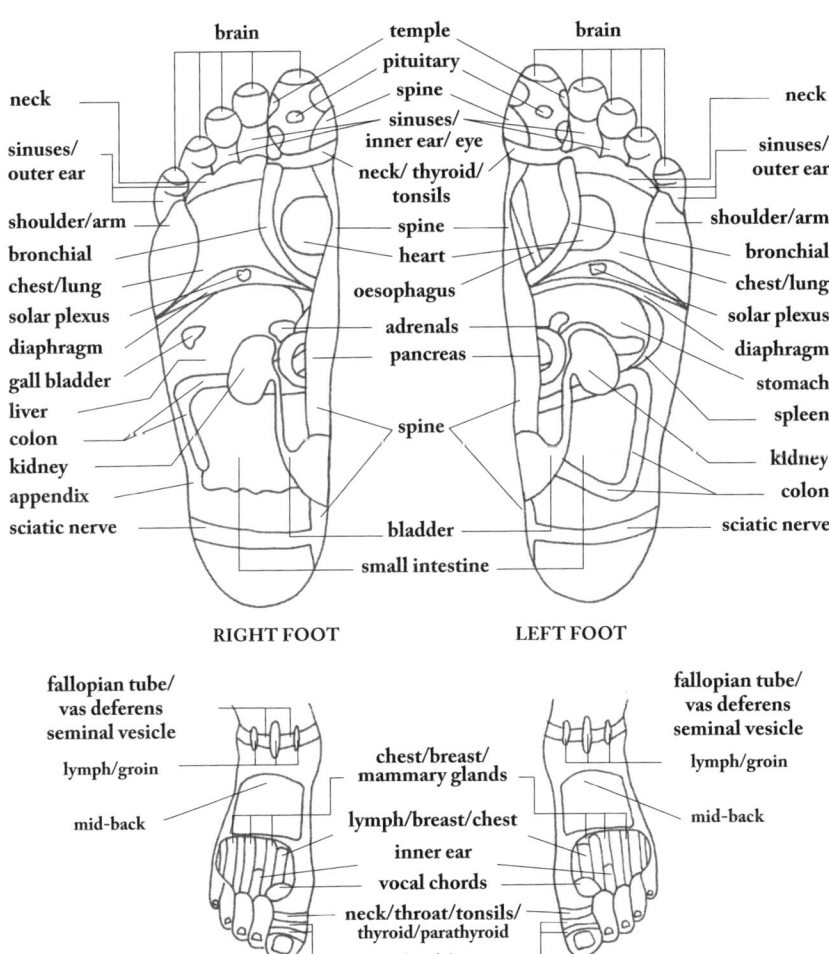

BOTAK CHIN: PROFILE OF AN INFAMOUS MALAYSIAN GANGSTER

1951	Born in Kuala Lumpur on 3 March to a middle-class family. He was the fifth of 10 children. His father worked for Malayan Railways.
1964	Dropped out of school at the age of 13 due to lack of money. Found a job at the wholesale market on Maxwell Road, selling vegetables and earning RM40 a month. Met local gang members and decided that robbing was better than selling vegetables.
1969	Along with two other felons, he staged his first robbery in April in Jinjang. With his portion of the spoils, he bought a gun. Committed eight more robberies with his gang before being caught in October 1969 and sentenced to 12 years in prison. On appeal, the sentence was reduced to seven years.
1969	Along with two other felons, he staged his first robbery in April in Jinjang. With his portion of the spoils, he bought a gun. Committed eight more robberies with his gang before being caught in October 1969 and sentenced to 12 years in prison. On appeal, the sentence was reduced to seven years.
1974	Released from prison. Went back to selling vegetables at the wholesale market, earning RM120 a month.
1975	Formed a four-man gang and bought more guns. Started a spree of robberies by hitting a gambling den in Setapak, taking away RM5,800. Committed at least 28 robberies, taking home approximately RM500,000 in spoils. Some of this money went to support the lavish lifestyle that he and his fellow gang members enjoyed. A portion of the proceeds, however, went to charity and the needy. This explains why, in certain quarters, he was known as a sort of "Robin Hood".
1975	Murdered two other gang members in Segambut, Kuala Lumpur because they failed in their duties to the gang. Stalked and shot his bitter enemy, Deputy Superintendent of Police S. Kulasingham in Kuala Lumpur. Kulasingham was rushed to the hospital and survived.
1976	Sent a wreath to the family of Tun Abdul Razak when the Prime Minister died.
1976	Ambushed by police while hiding with other gang members in a sawmill on Jalan Ipoh in Kuala Lumpur. Two gang members were shot dead, but Botak Chin and two others were arrested.
1980	Convicted and sentenced to death for illegal possession of firearms by the High Court.
1981	Stabbed three prison wardens in a foiled escape attempt.
1981	After eating his last meal comprising Kentucky Fried Chicken, fried mee (noodles), fruit and water, Botak Chin was hanged at 3 am on 11 June 1981.

Source: Adapted from *Insider's Kuala Lumpur* by Lam Seng Fatt, 2004

BEST-SELLING ALBUM

The Malaysian *nasyid* (Islamic-oriented music) group Raihan holds the record for the best-selling local album: 700,000 units of their *Puji-Pujian* album in 1996.

Source: *New Straits Times*

CABLE CODES FOR THE USE OF INTENDED VISITORS

Established by the Sarkies brothers in 1885, the Eastern and Oriental (E&O) Hotel in Penang has played host to famous guests such as Noel Coward, Douglas Fairbanks, Hermann Hesse, Rudyard Kipling, Sun Yat-Sen, Charlie Chaplin and Somerset Maugham. The following are cable codes taken from an E&O print advertisement dated 1909.

BUNCH: Wire if you have any vacant rooms and how many…
BUGBEAR: Reserve one single room for…
BUGGY: Reserve two single rooms for…
BUGLEHORN: Reserve three single rooms for…
BUGLER: Reserve four single rooms for…
BUILDING: Reserve five single rooms for…
BULBOUS: Reserve six single rooms for…
BULGED: Reserve one double room for…
BULIMY: Reserve two double rooms for…
BULKINESS: Reserve three double rooms for…
BULLACE: Reserve four double rooms for…
BULLCALF: Reserve five double rooms for…
BULLDOG: Reserve six double rooms for…
BULLETIN: Reserve a single and a double room for…
BULLFINCH: Reserve two double and a single room for…
BULLFROG: Reserve three double and a single room for…
BULLIRAG: Reserve a double room with two beds for…
BULLOCK: Reserve two double rooms adjoining for…
BULLTROUT: Reserve two single rooms adjoining for…
BUMPER: Have a single horse and carriage waiting at the wharf for…
BUMKIN: Have a carriage and pair waiting at the wharf for…
BUMPTIOUS: Runner to look after baggage…

SHOPPING TIPS: HOW TO TELL IF BATIK IS HAND-PAINTED

- **Look at the batik's design.** If the pattern is repetitive and symmetrical, the batik is probably made from block printing and not hand-painted.
- **Turn the batik over.** If you can see the pattern clearly, the batik is hand-painted. Block printing will only appear on one side of the cloth.
- **Smell the batik.** Hand-painted batik often has a particular fragrance due to the special roots, leaves and woods used to colour the materials.
- **Feel the material.** If the batik is silk, it is hand-painted. Other fabrics, such as cotton, may be used in both hand painting and block printing.
- **Check the price.** A hand-painted batik is typically much more expensive than a block-printed one. However, beware of unscrupulous sellers who will mark up the price of block-printed batiks in order to dupe customers.

DAYAK PRAYER TO HEAL A SICK CHILD

O white chicken, good chicken,
Chicken that is just a chick, crying peep-peep.
Throw off, send away Bale Oke, spirit of sores,
Bale Pali, spirit of sudden bad changes.
Release sickness from the body, from inside the body
Where it has gone deep, deaf to our call·
O white chicken, good chicken,
Chicken that is just a chick, crying peep-peep.
Sickness, follow the pig, the male pig
To the end of the mountain,
To the end of the valley, to the end of the mountain slope,
To the end of the steep slope on the mountain.
Beat the air from out of, get rid of, release·
You rhinoceros hornbill·
Beat the air out of, get rid of
The sickness from the body;
Break its hold on this life.

Source: *The Honey Tree Song* by Carol Rubenstein, 1985

SURVEYS OF MALAYSIANS FOUND THAT...

94% of lawyers surveyed thought that judicial authorities were susceptible to accepting bribes to give favourable judgments. (Transparency International Malaysia, 2008)

84% of the emails originating from Malaysia are spam. (*The Star*, 2007)

79% believe a person is defined by what he or she does for a living. (Synovate Sdn Bhd, 2008)

78% of bloggers were Chinese, 19% were Malays, 2% were Indians and 1% others. (Blogging and Democratization in Malaysia, 2006)

77% of consumers would be cutting back their spending in 2009. (*The Star*, 2008)

64% of consumers say they take notice of the nutritional information on food packaging. (AGB Nielsen Media Research, 2008)

58% of Chinese, 23% of Indians and 14% of Malays admitted to paying bribes. (Transparency International Malaysia, 2007)

46% think they are overweight and 58% are on a mission to lose weight. (AGB Nielsen Media Research, 2009)

45% think the Malaysian economy will improve in 2010. (Synovate Sdn Bhd, 2009)

44% shower right before going to bed. (*The Star*, 2009)

43% cite the state of the economy as their greatest concern followed by political stability (32%) and increasing food prices (18%). (AGB Nielsen Media Research, 2008)

40% are immune to the news, agreeing that they "find the economy boring and don't pay much attention". (Synovate Sdn Bhd, 2009)

12% do not have any savings from their monthly income. (Citibank Financial Quotient 2008 survey)

8% of drivers have bad eyesight. (*The Star*, 2006)

5% will let their body fight an illness and do not take medicine at all. (AGB Nielsen Media Research, 2008)

THE IBAN LONGHOUSE

Ruai
Gallery open on three sides, used by members of the longhouse community as a thoroughfare and gathering place. Large wooden mortars, firewood, tethered fighting cocks and hanging, blackened trophy heads can be found in the *ruai*. At night, the *ruai* serves as a sleeping quarters for boys, unmarried men and male visitors.

Sadau
Loft located above the *bilik* and *ruai* where the *padi* as well as other family possessions are stored. Young, unmarried women often sleep in the *sadau*.

Tanju
Open hardwood deck adjacent to the *ruai* and joined to all sections of the longhouse to form an unbroken raised platform. The *tanju* is where *padi* is dried before being stored in bark bins in the *sadau*.

Bilik
Private living quarters in which each individual family cooks, eats and sleeps. Each *bilik* is separated from other *bilik* and the *ruai* by walls, typically made of wooden planks.

LIFE EXPECTANCY IN YEARS

	1957	1970	1980	1990	2000	2007	2020
Male	55.8	61.6	66.4	68.9	70.2	71.7	72.6
Female	58.2	65.6	70.5	73.5	75.0	76.5	77.1

Source: Department of Statistics Malaysia

Birth rites

- The newborn is carried from the family apartment to the open-air veranda of the longhouse, where he is shown the sky and daylight for the first time.
- A pinch of salt is placed in the newborn's mouth to awaken his sense of taste.
- The elder holding the newborn utters an invocation to the gods.
- Three offerings are prepared for the family spirits, water spirits and forest spirits.
- Accompanied by the music of drums and gongs, the residents of the longhouse form a procession and make a complete circuit of the longhouse, strewing popped rice as they go, and make their way to the bathing place by the river.

Death rites

- The body of the deceased is carried to the centre of the family's room (bilik) in the longhouse and placed on the wooden floor which is slatted to allow water to flow through it.
- The body is bathed and dressed and then three dots of turmeric are painted on its forehead.
- As the body is carried through the doorway of the bilik to the ruai (gallery), family members shower it with grains of rice.
- The body is placed near a fire in a lower gallery inside a rectangular enclosure made of ritual ikat cloth.
- Throughout the night, a female dirge singer sits next to the body and sings the poem of lamentation to accompany the soul of the dead on its journey to the next world.
- At dawn, the body of the deceased is taken out of the longhouse and buried in a cemetery.

Source: Adapted from *Posts, Hearths and Thresholds: The Iban Longhouse as a Ritual Structure* by Clifford Sather, 1993

WET, WET, WET

Mean annual rainfall in Malaysia	3,085 mm
Annual rainfall at Bintulu, Sarawak (the wettest spot in Malaysia) in 2020	4,067.8 mm
Annual rainfall at Chuping, Perlis (the driest spot in Malaysia) in 2008	1,362 mm

Source: Malaysian Meteorological Department

THE TITLE OF "TUN"

"Tun" is the most senior federal title. There are two classes of the award: Seri Maharaja Mangku Negara and Seri Setia Mahkota

Seri Maharaja Mangku Negara (SMN)
Created on 6 August 1958, this award is given to deserving figures who have contributed greatly to the nation over a significant period of time.

Recipient	Gender	Position	Year awarded
Tuanku Kurshiah	♀	Raja Permaisuri Agong	1958
Colonel Henry Hau Shik Lee	♂	M	1958
Dr Tan Cheng Lock	♂	Founder of the MCA	1958
Leong Yew Koh	♂	YDP, Malacca	1958
Raja Uda Raja Muhammad	♂	YDP, Penang	1958
Tengku Ismail	♂	CP of Johor	1958
Tengku Munawir	♂	Reg of Negeri Sembilan	1958
Tuanku Yahya Petra	♂	Reg of Kelantan	1959
Tengku Budriah	♀	Raja Perempuan of Perlis	1959
Abdul Razak Hussein	♂	DPM	1959
Abdul Malek Yusof	♂	YDP, Malacca	1961
Mustafa Datu Harun	♂	YDP, Sabah	1964
Abang Haji Openg Abang Sapiee	♂	YDP, Sarawak	1964
Haji Ahmad Raffae	♂	YDP, Sabah	1967
Syed Sheh Syed Abdulah Shahabuddin	♂	YDP, Penang	1968
Tuanku Hj. Bujang Tuanku Haji Othman	♂	YDP, Sarawak	1970
Syed Sheh Syed Hassan Barakbah	♂	YDP, Penang	1970
Sharifah Rodziah Syed Ali Barakbah	♀	Wife of former PM	1970
Dr Haji Abdul Aziz Haji Abdul Majid	♂	YDP, Malacca	1972
Haji Muhammad Fuad Stephens	♂	YDP, Sabah	1975
Haji Sardon Haji Jubir	♂	YDP, Penang	1976
Syed Zahiruddin Syed Hassan	♂	YDP, Malacca	1976
Mohd. Hamdan Abdullah	♂	YDP, Sabah	1977
Ahmad Koroh	♂	YDP, Sabah	1978
Abang Muhammad Salahuddin	♂	YDP, Sarawak	1978
Mohamad Adnan Robert	♂	YDP, Sabah	1979
Hussein Onn	♂	Former PM	1981
Dr Awang Hassan	♂	YDP, Penang	1982
Dr Haji Abdul Rahman Yaakub	♂	YDP, Sarawak	1982
Tunku Ibrahim Ismail	♂	CP of Johor	1987

Recipient	Gender	Position	Year awarded
Syed Ahmad Syed Mahmud Shahabudin	♂	YDP, Malacca	1989
Muhammad Said Keruak	♂	YDP, Sabah	1989
Hj. Ahmad Zaidi Adruce Mohammed Noor	♂	YDP, Sarawak	1989
Dr Haji Hamdan Sheikh Tahir	♂	YDP, Penang	1989
Haji Sakaran Dandai	♂	YDP, Sabah	1996
Abdul Rahman Abbas	♂	YDP, Penang	2001
Ahmad Shah Abdullah	♂	YDP, Sabah	2003
Dr Mahathir Mohamad	♂	Former PM	2003
Dr Haji Mohd. Khalil Yaakob	♂	YDP, Malacca	2004
Abdullah Ahmad Badawi	♂	Former PM	2009
Juhar bin Haji Mahiruddin	♂	Yang di-Pertua Negeri Sabah ke-10	2011
Abdul Taib bin Mahmud	♂	Yang di-Pertua Negeri Sarawak ke-7	2014
Mohd Ali Rustam	♂	Yang di-Pertua Negeri Melaka ke-7	2020
Ahmad Fuzi Abdul Razak	♂	Yang di-Pertua Negeri Pulau Pinang ke-8	2021

Seri Setia Mahkota (SSM)
Created on 15 April 1966, this award is given to deserving figures who have contributed greatly to the nation.

Recipient	Gender	Position	Year awarded
Dr Ismail Datuk Haji Abdul Rahman	♂	DPM	1966
Sambanthan V.T	♂	M	1967
Tan Siew Sin	♂	M	1967
Syed Sheh Syed Hassan Barakbah	♂	LP	1968
Azmi Mohamed	♂	LP	1970
Mohd. Suffian Hashim	♂	LP	1975
Hajjah Rahah Tan Sri Haji Mohd. Noah	♀	Wife of former PM	1976
Haji Omar Ong Yoke Lin	♂	Sp, DN	1979
Ismail Mohd. Ali	♂	Former governor, Bank Negara Malaysia	1981
Temenggung Jugah	♂	M	1981
Dr Syed Nasir Ismail	♂	Sp, DR	1982
Raja Azlan Shah	♂	LP	1983
Haji Mohamed Salleh Abas	♂	LP	1985
Syed Ahmad Syed Mahmud Shahabudin	♂	YDP, Malacca	1987
Hj. Ahmad Zaidi Adruce Mohammed Noor	♂	YDP, Sarawak	1987

Recipient	Gender	Position	Year awarded
Abdul Hamid Haji Omar	♂	LP	1989
Suhailah Tan Sri Haji Mohd. Noah	♀	Wife of former PM	1990
Dr Lim Chong Eu	♂	Former chief minister of Penang	1991
Daim Zainuddin	♂	Former M	1991
Raja Mohar Raja Badiozaman	♂	Special economic adviser to the PM	1992
Mohammed Hanif Omar	♂	IGP	1993
Abdul Ghafar Baba	♂	Former M	1995
Mohd. Eusoff Chin	♂	CJ of Malaysia	1997
Mohamed Zahir Haji Ismail	♂	Sp, DR	1998
General (Rtd.) Haji Ibrahim Ismail	♂	Chief of defence forces	2000
Sulaiman Ninam Shah	♂	Permanent chairman, UMNO	2000
Mohamed Dzaiddin Hj. Abdullah	♂	CJ of Malaysia	2002
Abdullah Mohd. Salleh	♂	Senior administrative officer	2003
Fatimah Haji Hashim	♀	Former M	2003
Dr Siti Hasmah Haji Mohd. Ali	♀	Wife of former PM	2003
Dr Ling Liong Sik	♂	Former M	2004
Ahmad Fairuz Dato' Sheikh Abdul Halim	♂	CJ of Malaysia	2005
Dr Haji Muhammad Ghazali Shafie	♂	Former M	2005
Musa Hitam	♂	Former M	2006
Abdul Hamid Haji Mohamad	♂	CJ of Malaysia	2008
Ahmad Sarji Abdul Hamid	♂	Former chief secretary to the government	2008
Lim Keng Yaik	♂	Former M	2008
Jeanne Abdullah	♀	Wife of former PM	2009
Zaki Tun Azmi	♂	CJ of Malaysia	2009
Allahyarhamah Tun Endon Mahmood	♀	Isteri Tun Abdullah Ahmad Badawi	2009
Tun Azizan Zainul Abidin	♂	Presiden PETRONAS	2010
Tun Abdullah Ayub	♂	Ketua Setiausaha Perbendaharaan Malaysia	2011
Tun Arifin Zakaria	♂	Ketua Hakim Negara	2012
Tun Tan Sri Dato' Seri Md Raus Sharif	♂	Ketua Hakim Negara	2017
Tun Tan Sri Dato' Michael Chen Wing Sum	♂		
Tun Samy Vellu Sangalimuthu	♂		
Tun Tengku Maimun Tuan Mat	♀	Ketua Hakim Negara	2020

Recipient	Gender	Position	Year awarded
Tun Arshad Ayub	♂	Pro Canselor Universiti Teknologi Mara	2020
Tun Richard Malanjum	♂	bekas Ketua Hakim Negara	2020
Raja Tun Muhammad Alias Raja Muhammad Ali	♂	bekas Pengerusi Kumpulan Lembaga Kemajuan Tanah Persekutuan	2021
Tun Mohamed Hashim Mohd Ali	♂	bekas Ketua Turus Angkatan Tentera Malaysia	2022

CJ = chief justice
CP = crown prince
DN = Dewan Negara (Senate)
DPM = deputy prime minister
DR = Dewan Rakyat (House of Representatives)
IGP = inspector-general of police
LP = lord president
M = minister
MCA = Malaysian Chinese Association
PM = prime minister
Reg = regent
Sp = speaker
UMNO = United Malays National Organisation
YDP = Yang di-Pertua Negeri

Source: Jabatan Perdana Menteri

THE "MC" LEGAL BATTLE

In September 2009, United States fast food giant McDonald's lost an eight-year legal battle to prevent local Indian restaurant McCurry—located on Jalan Ipoh in Kuala Lumpur—from using the "Mc" prefix on its business signage. In 2001, McDonald's had filed a suit claiming that the local restaurant was misrepresenting itself and wrongfully associating itself with the fast food franchise. The High Court ruled in 2006 that McDonald's did have the exclusive right to the prefix "Mc" and ordered McCurry to pay damages to McDonald's for trademark infringement, but that decision was subsequently reversed by the Court of Appeal in April 2009. The Court of Appeal said that the McCurry menu (strictly Indian food) and signboard (white and grey letters against red background with a picture of a smiling chicken giving a double thumbs-up) were distinctly different from McDonald's, and that the franchise could not have a monopoly on the "Mc" prefix in Malaysia. McCurry owner P. Suppiah gleefully stuck the letter "c" back onto the signboard of his shop, which had been known as "M Curry" since 2001. The Federal Court later dismissed an appeal by McDonald's and ordered the franchise to pay RM10,000 to McCurry.

Source: *The Star*

FIRST IMPRESSIONS OF THE MALAY ARCHIPELAGO

From the diary of James Brooke, who became the first White Rajah of Sarawak in 1841.

> 1 August 1839
>
> 'Today at noon, we distinctly made out the main land of Borneo; and, steering a course for the low point of Tanjong Api, anchored, amidst squalls of thunder, lightning, and rain. At length, then, I am on the coast of Borneo. Our work is commenced. I have toiled and sacrificed much for this consummation; and, now that it has arrived, I ask myself if I feel equal to the task... My feelings I can hardly describe. They are not those of tumultuous joy at the prospect of success; but, on the contrary, are rather of a composed and quiet nature; a fixed determination to gird up my loins and endeavour to effect an object and to perform a service which may be useful to mankind and creditable to myself; whilst, at the same time, I must constantly bear in mind that every step I take must inevitably be fraught with difficulties and dangers.'

An account of the voyage of Yap Ah Loy, the Kapitan Cina and founder of Kuala Lumpur, from China to Malaya in 1854 at the age of 17.

> 'At Macao he embarked in a junk, and voyaged out over the deep, wide ocean. The junk sailed to Malaya. He was full of hope, though his property consisted of no more than eighty dollars in Chinese currency and a few cheap pieces of luggage. The junk sailed for more than a month, and passed through many dangers, before it reached Malacca. When at last he landed he found himself in a place very different from China. The scenery, with the tall coconut and betel palms and the small attap houses, was new and attractive to him. The unhappy time he had experienced during the long voyage was totally forgotten. He was as peaceful and at ease as the blue sky over the Southern ocean.'
>
> — From *The Biography of Yap Ah Loy*, 1951

J.W.W. BIRCH'S LAST JOURNAL ENTRIES

On 2 November 1875, the first British Resident of Perak, J.W.W. Birch, was speared to death by an Orang Asli, acting on behalf of a local Malay chief, while bathing nearby a river in Pasir Salak, Perak.

---

23 October 1875, Saturday

It rained very heavily from 4 am. to 6 am. It then cleared and began again from 1 pm. until 4 pm. By that time the river had risen 1 foot here. All efforts to find my letters and other missing things failed.

Bacon, whom I had sent down to Kotastia about materials, came back. He had seen Laxamana and Laxamana told him he was now very sad in spirit—all his power was gone and he could no longer punish anyone, but he was quite willing to serve under the British and he hoped that I would employ him. Mr Bacon said when you were at Blanja had you signed I am certain you would have had an allowance. Now I believe you will get nothing unless you are employed, and when Mr Birch asked you the other day to sign and be employed, you send no reply to him but said you would come and never did. He said well I am really coming now. I will be there tomorrow or the next day.

It rained again very badly in the afternoon, and from time to time during the night.

---

24 October 1875, Sunday

Very cold in the morning. Got the boats all moored, as water was rapidly rising. Rain very heavy in morning and showery all day. Several men of Perak came and engaged themselves to take jungle at as fixed price. Raja Te' of Bendimin behind here came and asked to cut timber for me and on what terms. I accepted his terms at once for my house, which I am very anxious to finish.

Source: *The Journals of J.W.W. Birch, First British Resident to Perak, 1874–1875*

THE SCOUT ASSOCIATION OF MALAYSIA

Each of the 73,494 (as of 2008) Scout Association of Malaysia members had to pledge to adhere to the following **Scout Laws**:

1. A Scout's honour is to be trusted.
2. A Scout is loyal.
3. A Scout's duty is to be useful and to help others.
4. A Scout is a friend to all and a brother to every other Scout.
5. A Scout is courteous.
6. A Scout is a friend to animals.
7. A Scout obeys orders of his parents, Patrol Leader or Scoutmaster without question.
8. A Scout smiles and whistles under all difficulties.
9. A Scout is thrifty.
10. A Scout is clean in thought, word and deed.

> **A Malaysian Scout Song**
> O Semangat
>
> Chorus:
>
> O Semangat O Semangat,
> We know why we are happy,
> Scouting spirit, scouting spirit,
> That makes us always happy.
>
> We are scouts from all Malaysia,
> Different races different tongues,
> Always smiling full of cheer,
> We want to come back every year.
>
> Cooking food and playing games,
> We must keep the camp site neat,
> Round the campfire song we sing,
> We find our happiness complete.

Founding of the Scout Troops

Year	State	Founders
1908	Penang	YMCA Experimental Troop
1909	Selangor	B. E. Shaw (Victoria Institution)
1912	Pahang	George Muir Laidlaw Restored in 1927 by Henry Reginald Hertslet
1913	Sarawak	Reverend Thomas Cecil Alexander (St Thomas's School, Kuching)
1915	North Borneo (Sabah)	Reverend Thomas Cecil Alexander
1915	Penang	Harold A. R. Cheeseman (Penang Free School)
1922	Kedah	E.C. Hicks, E.A.G. Stuart, R.P.S. Walker and C.W. Bloomfield (Sultan Abdul Hamid College)
1923	Negeri Sembilan	Edward Shaw (Seremban)
1926	Perak	L. R. Wheeler (Malay College, Kuala Kangsar)
1926	Malacca	R. Brunstone

1927	Kelantan	Y.M. Tengku Ahmad Temenggong
1928	Johor	Harold A. R. Cheeseman (English College, Johore Bahru)
1929	Terengganu	Alan James Gracie
1931	Perlis	Basil Hugh Roger-Smith

STUDYING ABROAD

Number of Malaysian students who studied at foreign institutions of higher learning:

Country	2003	2005	2007	2016	2019
Australia	15,448	15,909	13,010	20,493	—
United Kingdom and Ireland	11,860	15,189	11,490	13,796	7,709
Egypt	4,330	6,256	6,896	8,611	—
United States of America	7,611	6,411	5,281	6,100	—
Indonesia	1,225	2,444	4,565	5,588	—
New Zealand	918	1,338	1,574	2,305	—
Jordan	361	444	655	unk	730
Canada	231	230	312	unk	—
Saudi Arabia	125	132	125	unk	—
Taiwan	—	—	—	5,133	—
China	—	—	—	2,792	—
Russia	—	—	—	2,521	—
India	—	—	—	2,175	—
Others	n/a	8,256	11,007	—	—

Total 59,144*

* Total for 2021
Source: Ministry of Higher Education Malaysia

WHAT'S IN A NAME?

Cameron Highlands (Pahang)
Famed for its tea plantations, Cameron Highlands was named after William Cameron, a British colonial government surveyor who discovered the highlands during a mapping expedition in 1885

Cheras (Selangor)
Cheras is a satellite town south of Kuala Lumpur. The word "Cheras" may have been derived from the Malay words *tras* or *teras*, referring to the hardest part of a tree trunk. The Chinese called Cheras "Chiu-Lai" after the large banana plantations there.

Damansara (Selangor)
The name Damansara could be derived from a port on the Gombak River, which was called "Labohan Sara". *Labohan* means a place where ships may anchor and *sara*, a word used for people on a pension, may have carried the meaning of leaving, departure or embarkation. The name Damansara could also be derived from the Indian words *daman* and *sara*. The former word in Hindustani means "foothills", which is a correct description of the area, while *sara* in Sanskrit means "water" and in Hindustani "a mansion of wealth".

Fraser's Hill (Pahang)
A hill resort, Fraser's Hill derives its name from Louis James Fraser, a solitary Scottish pioneer who set up a tin-ore trading post in Pahang in the 1890s.

Kampung L.B. Johnson (Negeri Sembilan)
Also known as Felda L.B. Johnson, this FELDA settlement was named the then U.S. President Lyndon B. Johnson, who visited the village in 1966.

Kampung New Zealand (Pahang)
New Zealand donated 550,000 Malaysian dollars and provided experts for the development of this 2,650-acre rubber plantation that is situated off the East–West highway. Appropriately, the new kampong was named in its honour.

Port Dickson (Negeri Sembilan)
Port Dickson is named after Sir Frederick Dickson, who was colonial secretary and acting governor of the colony in 1890.

Prai (Penang)
According to one theory, Prai was named after *kain perai*, a black silk cloth Malays use at daybreak to protect themselves from the damp morning air. Another explanation is that the name Prai is derived from the words *berperai-perai* meaning "breaking up in all directions", a reference to the silt brought up to the estuary of the Prai River.

Source: *Place-Names in Peninsular Malaysia* by Durai Raja Singam, 1980, *Notes on the Historical Geography of Malaya and Sidelights on the Malay Annals* by Dato F.W. Douglas, 1949, *Going Places*

UNDER PENALTY OF DEATH

Under Malaysian law, the death penalty is mandatory for certain offences and discretionary for others.

Mandatory death penalty

Offence	Law that provides for the death penalty
Trafficking or offering to traffic in dangerous drugs	Section 39(B) of the Dangerous Drugs Act 1952
Discharging a firearm in the commission of a scheduled offence	Section 3 of the Firearms (Increased Penalties) Act 1971
Being an accomplice in a case of discharging of a firearm	Section 3A of the Firearms (Increased Penalties) Act 1971
Offences in security areas for possession of firearms, ammunition and explosives	Section 57(1) of the Internal Security Act 1960
Offences against the person of the Yang di-Pertuan Agong, Ruler or Yang di-Pertua Negeri	Section 121(A) of the Penal Code
Murder	Section 302 of the Penal Code
Attempt to murder (if hurt is caused)	Section 307(2) of the Penal Code
Rape resulting in death	Section 376(3) of the Penal Code
Hostage taking resulting in death	Section 374(A) of the Penal Code
Terrorist act resulting in death	Section 130(C) of the Penal Code

Discretionary death penalty

Offence	Law that provides for the death penalty
Abduction, wrongful restraint or wrongful confinement for ransom (kidnapping)	Section 3(1) of the Kidnapping Act 1961
Consorting with a person carrying or having possession of firearms, ammunition or explosives in a security area	Section 58(1) of the Internal Security Act 1960
Waging or attempting to wage war or abetting the waging of war against the Yang di-Pertuan Agong, a Ruler or Yang di-Pertua Negeri	Section 121 of the Penal Code
Gang-robbery with murder	Section 396 of the Penal Code
Abetment of suicide of a child, an insane or delirious person, an idiot, or intoxicated person	Section 305 of the Penal Code
Abetment of mutiny within the Malaysian Armed Forces	Section 132 of the Penal Code
Kidnapping or abducting in order to murder	Section 364 of the Penal Code

Source: Various sections and acts of Malaysian laws

A SELECTION OF MALAYSIAN GOVERNMENT SLOGANS

Slogan	Translation
Bahasa Jiwa Bangsa	Language Is The Soul Of The Nation
Bangsa Malaysia	Malaysian Nation
Berhati-Hati Di Jalan Raya	Be Careful On The Road
Bekerja Dengan Saya, Bukan Untuk Saya	Work With Me, Not For Me
Belia Benci Dadah	Youth Hate Drugs
Belilah Barangan Buatan Malaysia	Buy Malaysian-made Goods
Bersatu Kita Teguh, Bercerai Kita Roboh	United We Stand, Divided We Fall
Bersih, Cekap Dan Amanah	Clean, Efficient, Trustworthy
Budi Bahasa Budaya Kita	Courtesy Is Our Culture
Buy British Last	—
Cemerlang, Gemilang, Terbilang	Excellence, Glory, Distinction
Cinta IT, Sayang IT	Love IT, Love IT
Cintailah Bahasa Kebangsaan Kita	Love Our National Language
Cintailah Sungai Kita	Love Our Rivers
Cuti-Cuti Malaysia	Holidays In Malaysia
Jauhi Diri Anda Dari Dadah	Keep Away From Drugs
Kebersihan Tanggungjawab Bersama	Cleanliness Is Our Responsibility
Kepimpinan Melalui Teladan	Leadership By Example
Keranamu Malaysia	Because Of You Malaysia
Hapuskan Denggi	Destroy Dengue
Hargailah Alam Sekitar Kita	Appreciate Our Environment
Majulah Sukan Untuk Negara	Develop Sports For The Nation
Malaysia Boleh!	Malaysia Can Do It!
Malaysia. Truly Asia	—
Mesra, Cepat, Betul	Friendly, Efficient and Right
Negara Bersih, Rakyat Sihat	Clean Country, Healthy Citizens
Masyarakat Penyayang	Caring Society

Tahun Melawat Malaysia	Visit Malaysia Year
Pandu Cermat Jiwa Selamat	Drive Carefully, Save Lives
Pandu Dengan Cermat, Ingatlah Orang Tersayang	Drive Carefully, Remember Your Loved Ones
Rakyat Didahulukan, Pencapaian Diutamakan	People First, Performance Now
Rumahku, Syurgaku	My Home, My Paradise
Satu Malaysia	One Malaysia
Saya Anti Rasuah	I Am Against Corruption
Sekolahku, Rumahku	My School, My Home
Tak Nak!	Don't Want!
Wawasan 2020	Vision 2020

SOME MANGLISH SUFFIXES

Suffix	Meaning	English equivalent	Example
lah	To affirm a statement	Of course	Don't be lazy *lah*! He's the one *lah*! Don't worry *lah*.
nah	Used when handing something to another person	Here you go	Take this, *nah*!
liao	Used as a literal translation of "already"	Already	No stock *liao*. Finished *liao*.
meh	Used when asking questions, especially when a person is sceptical of something	Is that true?	Yeah *meh*?

THE INTENSITY OF THE CILI PADI

The piquancy of chillies is measured in Scoville heat units (SHU) via a method known as high-pressure liquid chromatography. The lowest rating on the Scoville scale, measured by bell peppers, is 0 SHU. By contrast, the world's hottest chilli—the Naga Jolokia, which grows in Bangladesh—has a Scoville rating of 1.04 million SHU, while standard US-grade pepper sprays measure between 2 million and 5.3 million SHU. The Malaysian *cili padi* has a rating of 50,000 to 100,000 SHU.

Minimum height requirement in centimetres for female flight attendants of Malaysia Airlines, AirAsia and Firefly:

INDEX

A

Abdul Rahman, Tunku 7, 9, 67, 76, 86, 89
Abdul Razak, Tun 7, 76, 86, 142
Abdullah Ahmad Badawi, Tun 71, 76, 86, 150
Abdul Talib Haron 93
A Famosa 130
AirAsia 30, 159
airplane crash 29
airport codes 122
Akademi Fantasia 47
Ananda Krishnan 20
architects 125
architectural symbolism 90
average monthly consumption 58

B

Badi Gajah 21
banana leaf rice 62
banned movies 42
Barber, Noel 66
batik 13, 48, 107, 144
Bentong Kali 34
best-selling local album 143
betel-chewing 104
Bidayuh headhunting songs 32
Birch, J.W.W. 128, 153
birds' nests 14, 74
Boh Cameronian Lifetime Achievement Award 60
bomoh 8, 10, 17, 28

Botak Chin 142
Borneo pygmy elephant identification 64
Borneo pygmy elephant recipe 43
Brooke, James 152
Bujang Valley 106, 119
burglaries 74

C

calories 105
Cameron Highlands 22, 120, 156
cannons 80
causes of death 94
chengal 8, 71
Cheong Fatt Tze mansion 89
Chinese foot reflexology 141
Chinese medicine 69
Chinese secret societies 40, 66, 99
Christ Church 56, 57, 106
cinema admissions 115
Communists 18, 27, 66, 91, 109
Conrad, Joseph 23
crazy toad 32
crows 107

D

Dayak prayer 144
De Albuquerque, Afonso 83
death penalty 55, 157
Department of Islamic Development Malaysia (JAKIM) 18
Dogs, breeds under import control 140

drug trafficking 55, 63, 130
durian 35, 43, 54, 68, 86, 94, 105, 112, 126

E

earlobe stretching 34
Eastern and Oriental (E&O) Hotel 137, 143
eating advice 35
eating with your fingers 66
elephants, how to catch a herd 31
elephant hunting 119
elephant insemination 9
English words borrowed from Malay 68

F

fast-food outlets 50
Feng Shui 89
fermented Malaysian foods 126
Film Censorship Board 42, 123
fire breakouts 108
first citizenship certificate holder 102
first Malayan film 114
first Malay professor 95
Five Foot Way 7
foreigners in the headlines 63
foreign films shot in Malaysia 96

G

gearbox soup 15
ghosts 44, 59, 130, 137
goat breeding 104

government operations 109
government slogans 158, 159
guidelines on naming children 28, 29

H

hand gestures 84
Hibiscus rosa-sinensis 38, 106
Hikayat Abdullah 31, 130
Hindu temple 10, 90
Hungry Ghost Festival 44
Hussein Onn, Tun 7, 76, 86, 148

I

Iban child naming 80
Iban design motifs 138
Iban longhouse 146, 147
identical twins 55
institutions of higher learning 155
Internal Security Act detainees 132
Islam 18, 19, 38, 41, 85, 90, 110, 132, 136, 143
Islamic divorce 102
Istana Budaya 129
Istana Negara 43, 106, 123
itinerary, Federated Malay States 91
itinerary, Spookster Ghost Tour 137

J

Jackson, Michael 13
Jah-Het 72
Jawi 37

Jewish cemetery 84

K

kacip fatimah 80
kampong house 8
kebaya 13, 39
Kelantanese advice 39
kites (wau) 9
knuckle strikes 45
kris 23, 51, 90
Kuala Lumpur Composite Index (KLCI) 52, 53

L

Laila Majnun 114
laksa 97
Langkasuka 135
Leaning Tower of Teluk Intan 24
licence plates 131
life expectancy 27, 146
Light, Francis 67
longest, the 59, 133
LRT 25, 89
Lubang Nasib Bagus cave 31

M

Mahathir Mohamad, Tun Dr 61, 76, 79, 86, 99, 109, 110, 149
Mah Meri 21
Malacca legends 118
Malacca tombstones 56, 57
Malacca townhouse 73
Malay (definition) 38
Malaya's most wanted 27
Malayan remedies 62
Malayan songbook 33

Malay body idioms 139
Malay ghosts 59
Malay insults 114
Malay proverbs 46
Malay words, origins 134
Malaysia Airlines 13, 29, 60, 115, 159
Malaysian Armed Forces 40, 41
Malaysian computers 118
Malaysian firsts 88, 89
Malaysian flag 64
Malaysian National Registration Department 28
Malaysian Philharmonic Orchestra 107
Malaysian royalty 28, 122
Malaysian Sign Language 8
Malaysian time 113
Malaysian world record achievers 121
Malaysians who have appeared on stamps 76, 77, 78
Manglish grammar 111
Manglish suffixes 159
marriages and divorces 25, 102
Maybank 30
McCurry 151
McDonald's 50, 151
mean monthly gross household income 95
medical malpractice 108
medicine bag 10
members' clubs 26
Menara Maybank 43, 68, 123, 125, 90
Minor Offences Act 15
mobile meals 36, 37
moonrat 24, 47
mortality rates 102
Mount Kinabalu 101
Mulu National Park 31, 106

murders 16, 17, 18
Muslim astronauts 18, 19
MyKad 126

N

Najib Tun Razak, Dato' Sri 7, 19, 25, 86
National Art Award 117
national heritage, tangible 106, 107
National Literary Award 117
National Monument 17, 106
National Mosque 75, 106, 123, 125
National Service Programme 15
Na Tuk Kong 118
Negaraku 124
Niah Caves 14
Nilai Memorial Park 113
notifiable diseases 140

O

orang-utans 11, 47, 53, 68, 129
Orang Asli 21, 24, 45, 55, 72, 127, 153
Orang Ulu 34

P

P. Ramlee 78, 103, 129
pantun 39
Penang Bridge 87, 133
performance problems 12, 13
Petronas 30, 150
Petronas Twin Towers 43, 68, 87, 101, 117, 123, 125
phone bill 79
place names 156
poisonous animals 44
political party admission fees 136
Poor Thamby Works On The Railway 72

population density 67, 138
population statistics 64
Port Klang 29, 89, 100
prime ministers' favourite foods 86
proboscis monkeys 115
prohibited company names 70
prohibited imagery in newspapers and magazines 92
Proton 133
Proton Saga 89, 98
public holidays 43
pulse reading 69

R

Raffles, Stamford 7
Raihan 143
rainfall 120, 147
Raja Permaisuri Agong 70, 122, 148
Ramly Burger 85
Ranee of Sarawak 23
remedies for fever 73
richest Malaysians 20, 21
rickshaw drivers 116
ringgit 15, 87, 93
rites of passage 48, 49
road accidents 29, 38
Robert Kuok 20
Royal Malay Regiment 29
Royal Selangor Club 26, 124

S

salaries of ministers and senior civil servants 79
Sarawak baskets 35
sarong 13, 39, 68, 101
satay 59, 68, 105, 134, 163

school mottos 82
Scout Association of Malaysia 154, 155
secret society poetry 66
sepak takraw 65
shadow puppet 45
Sheikh Muszaphar Shukor, Datuk 13, 78
Sidek serve 84
Sikhs 18
silat 14, 45, 101, 135
Siti Khadijah market 120
Sky Kingdom 60
skyscrapers 68, 87
Smart Tunnel 11
snakebite marks 136
Snake Temple 70
Spiderman 87
spitting 15
Sri Rama 45
Straits Settlements latrine 58
street names 128
subtitles 51
sultan of Malacca's palace 93
surveys of Malaysians 145
Swettenham, Frank 107, 128
swiftlet farm 133

T

tapirs 27, 47, 53, 78, 92
Tasik Chini 55
tattooing 27
tiger dining habits 92
tiger encounters 127
timber 22, 61, 71, 100, 121, 153
tin dredge 75
tongkat ali 80, 104
top spinning 55
torpedo soup 15
traditional weights and measures 81

train accidents 29
tsunami 29
tuak 30
Tun 148–151

U

undivided leaf 87
United Malays National Organisation (UMNO) 128, 136, 151
Ungku Abdul Aziz Ungku Abdul Hamid 95

V

valuable brands 30
vehicles 11, 36, 37, 39, 50, 67, 100, 131
venereal disease 104

W

weather 120
wildlife-related crimes and punishments 78
wine pairings 112
world record achievers 121
worst, the 29

X

Xavier, Saint Francis 118

Y

yam seng 48, 116
Yang di-Pertuan Agong 70, 117, 122, 128, 157
Yap Ah Loy 67, 137, 152

Z

Zoo Negara 11, 149